The Accelerator

The Theory-Fingerboard Connection

By
Howard Roberts
with
Charles Fechter
and
Keith Wyatt

Cover Design: K. Adolphsen

Copyright © 1980 by Howard M. Roberts
Published by Playback Music Publishing Inc. P.O. Box 15, Edmonds, Washington 98020
All Rights Reserved   Printed and Published in U.S.A.   International Copyright Secured

ISBN 0-89915-014-4

Foreword

Based on the authors' experience over the years dealing with thousands of aspiring guitarists in seminars and at the Guitar Institute of Technology, it has become increasingly clear that the single greatest handicap facing a student of the guitar is an unfamiliarity with the common language of music, i.e., not knowing the names of the notes, their scale step numbers in all keys, and their locations on the staff and on the fingerboard. (The problem is that the students don't know, for example, what the 3rd of G is and by the time they figure it out, the tune has left them behind; or, if they know that B is the note in question, they can't find it on the guitar in time. In either case, the process of playing music comes to a screeching halt.) Difficulty with specific things is unmistakably the proverbial banana peel for the vast majority of students having problems with subjects such as harmony, chord melody, arranging, and composition. Indeed, it could safely be said that to have a clear grasp of this information is to understand the language of music at the nuts and bolts level ("put the 3rd in the bass", "give me a III-VI-II-V progression in the key of Bb", "move those chords up in parallel fourths", "add a 9th on the top of that chord", and so the language goes, not only at the academic level but also in professional life.) You might say it's a word and number game and once understood, gives access to the language and thereby kicks open the door to any study of music in general and the guitar in specific, with a much accelerated learning curve. Because of this, we felt that this book needed to be written as a preparatory study guide for the incoming students of G.I.T.

Table of Contents

Chapter One

INSTRUCTION ONE:

There is a test at the end of Chapter One (page 24). Before you read Chapter One, take the test, following the instructions given. If you can complete the test *without mistakes, within the time limit*, you may go immediately to Instruction Two on page 26. If you cannot complete the test as prescribed, go back to the first page of Chapter One (page 6) and begin your study of the book there.

IMPORTANT: It doesn't matter how long it takes you to master the information in Chapter One; but you must eat and sleep this information until it is totally committed to memory. Do not go on to Chapter Two until you can complete the test at the end of Chapter One comfortably within the time limit. (45 minutes)

SECTION ONE

KNOW THE NAMES OF THE NOTES ON THE FIRST AND FOURTH STRINGS

By knowing the names of the notes on the first string, you can use the diagonal shape (dotted line) on Fig. 1 below as a visual aid to learn the names of the notes on the fourth string.

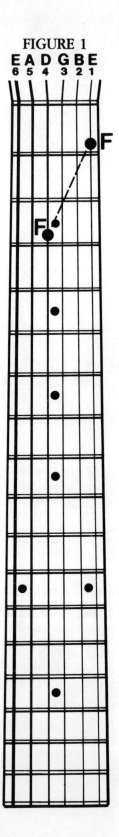

FIGURE 1

To memorize the names of the notes in Fig. 2 and their location on the fingerboard:

STEP 1: without the guitar, memorize the names of the notes on the first string.

STEP 2: Turn the page over and play the notes on the first string ascending and descending in pitch and saying the names aloud.

STEP 3: Memorize the names of the notes on the fourth string using the shape in **Fig. 1** as a visual aid.

STEP 4: Turn the page over and play the notes on the fourth string ascending and descending in pitch and saying the names aloud.

Now learn the names of the sharped and flatted notes (called "accidentals") on the first and fourth **strings** by repeating steps 1-4. (See Fig. 3) NOTE: D# and Eb are the same pitch—D# is the note D raised a half step and Eb is the note E lowered a half step. Know both names for this pitch and the other accidentals.

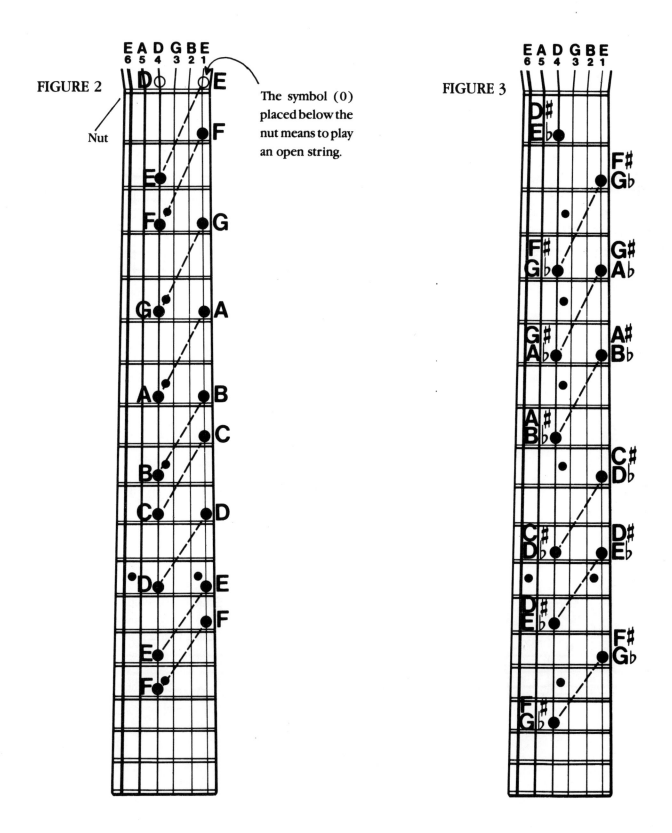

The symbol (0) placed below the nut means to play an open string.

7

SECTION TWO

PLAY THE MAJOR SCALE IN ALL KEYS

Memorize the major scale fingering pattern for the key of C as shown in Fig. 4 below. NOTE: the tonic tones (the "C's") are circled. The tonic is the alphabet name of the scale e.g. Bb is the tonic of the key of Bb etc.

In order to play the major scale in any other key, simply locate the tonic on the first and/or fourth strings and play the same pattern. See Fig. 5 for any example.

FIGURE 4

MAJOR SCALE FINGERING PATTERN
KEY OF C

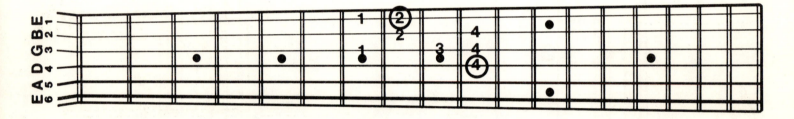

NOTE: Numbers on diagram show fingering.

FIGURE 5

MAJOR SCALE FINGERING PATTERN
KEY OF G

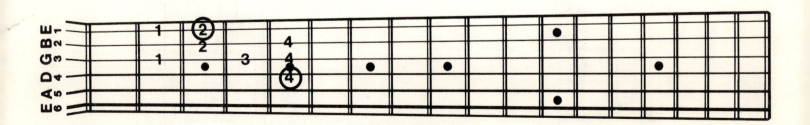

Using the major scale fingering pattern from Fig. 4, play the major scale in each of the keys below (memorize their locations on the fingerboard so you can locate them quickly). Using a metronome, play the scales ascending and descending, one note per beat. Make no mistake more than once. You can mistake-proof your practice by using a metronome setting slow enough to eliminate any possibility of error. IMPORTANT: hold each note as long as possible. Through practicing every day this way you will soon attain speed and smoothness of execution. SPEED IS THE BYPRODUCT OF ACCURACY.

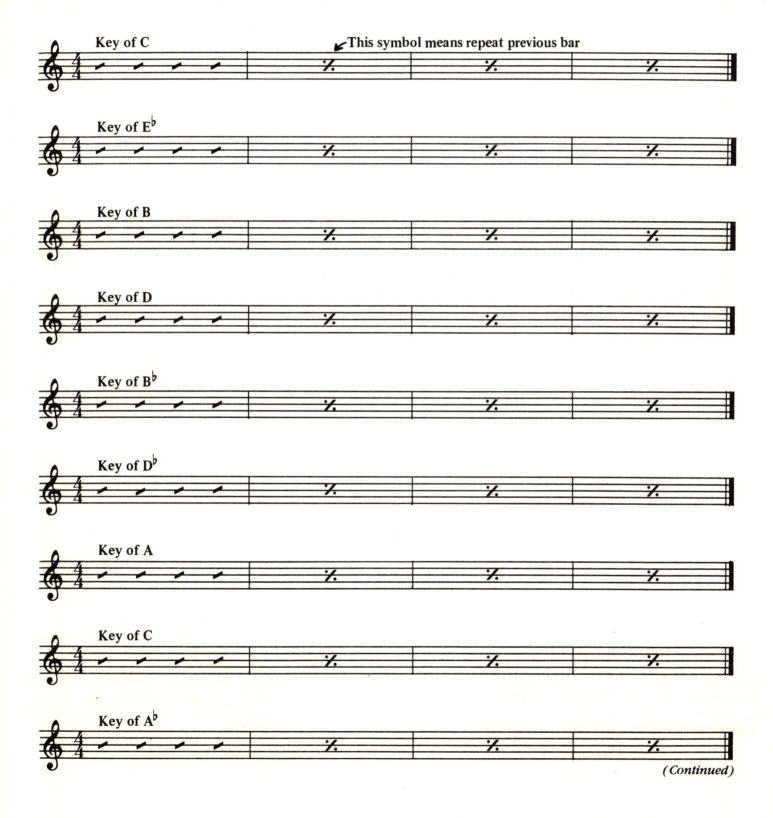

(Continued)

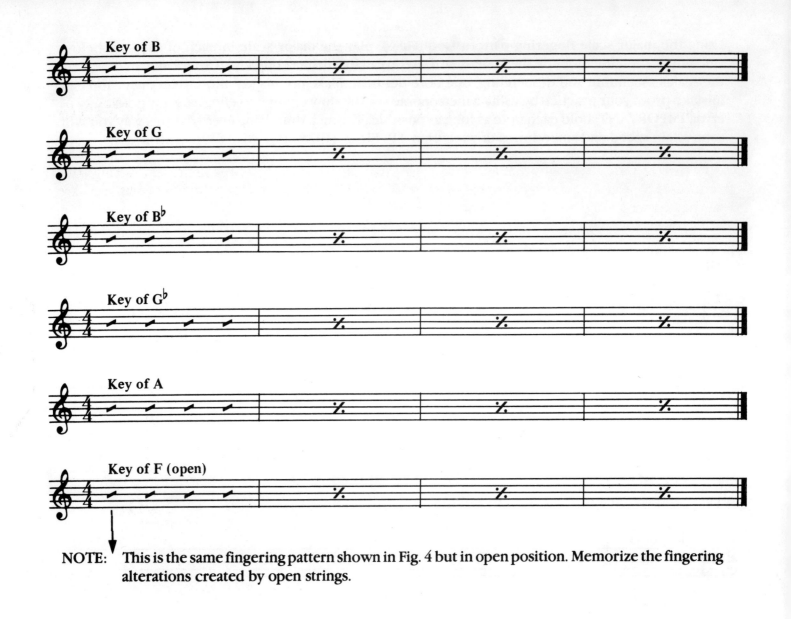

NOTE: This is the same fingering pattern shown in Fig. 4 but in open position. Memorize the fingering alterations created by open strings.

FIGURE 6

MAJOR SCALE FINGERING PATTERN (OPEN)
KEY OF F

SECTION THREE

KNOW THE NAMES OF THE NOTES ON THE SIXTH STRING

Referring to the figures shown below, memorize the names of all of the notes on the sixth string. This will be easy because the names are identical to the notes on the first string (same fret) that you have already learned in figures 1-3.

FIGURE 7

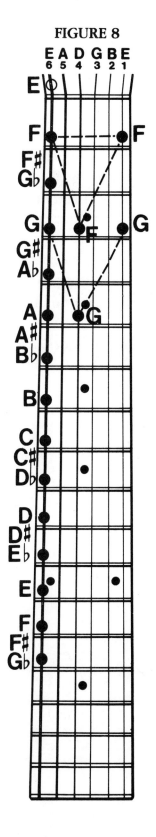

FIGURE 8

SECTION FOUR

PLAY A MINOR SEVENTH CHORD
(ROOT ON SIXTH STRING)

Memorize the D minor seventh chord shown in Fig. 9.

Note that the root of the chord (D) is on the sixth string (circled).

The root is the alphabet name of the chord, e.g. the root of G minor 7 is G; etc.

To play a C minor 7, play the same shape with the root on the sixth string, eighth fret.

(Note: "minor 7" is often abbreviated "m7" or "min 7").

FIGURE 9

Play the minor seventh chord through all the keys below, holding each chord for four beats on the metronome. Move from one chord to the next quickly and cleanly, holding each one as long as possible.

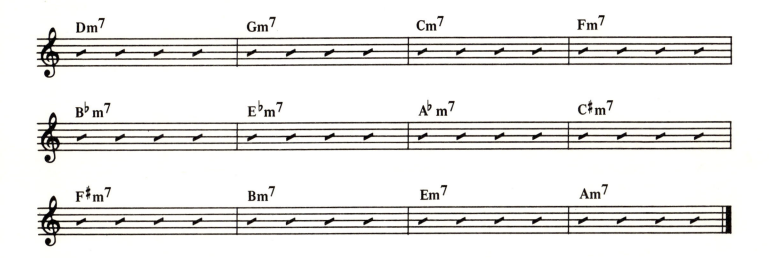

SECTION FIVE

PLAY A MAJOR SEVENTH CHORD
(ROOT ON THE SIXTH STRING)

Memorize the C major seventh chord shown in Fig. 10.

Note that the root is on the sixth string.

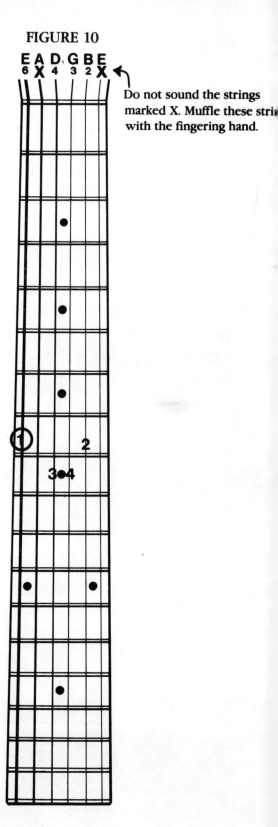

FIGURE 10

Do not sound the strings marked X. Muffle these strings with the fingering hand.

Play the major seventh chord through all the keys below using the same procedure as for the minor seventh chord. (NOTE: "C major seventh" is commonly abbreviated "C maj 7").

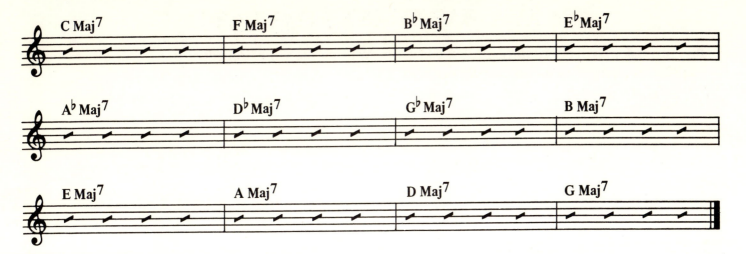

SECTION SIX

Memorize the C major sixth chord shown on Fig. 11 below.

FIGURE 11

Play the major sixth chord through all the keys below using the same procedure previously described. (NOTE: "C major 6" is commonly abbreviated "C6").

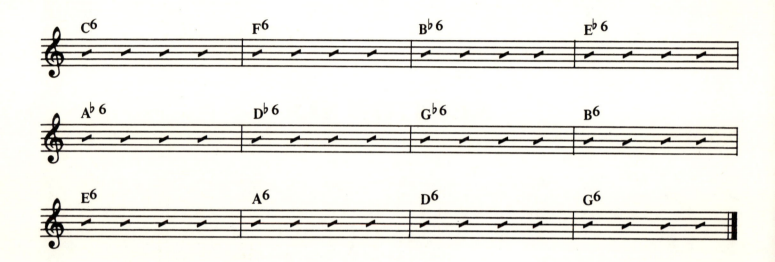

SECTION SEVEN

KNOW THE NAMES OF THE NOTES ON THE SECOND AND FIFTH STRINGS

By knowing the names of the notes on the second string, you can use the diagonal shape (dotted line) on Fig. 12 as a visual aid to learn the names of the notes on the fifth string.

FIGURE 12

To memorize the names of the notes in Fig. 13 and their location on the fingerboard:

STEP 1: without the guitar, memorize the names of the notes on the second string.

STEP 2: Turn the page over and play the notes on the first string ascending and descending.

STEP 3: Turn the page over and play the notes on the second string ascending and descending in pitch and saying the names aloud.

STEP 4: Memorize the names of the notes on the fifth string using the shape in Fig. 12 as a visual aid.

STEP 5: Turn the page over and play the notes on the fifth string ascending and descending in pitch and saying the names aloud.

Now learn the names of the accidentals on the second and fifth strings by repeating steps 1-5. See Fig. 14.

FIGURE 13

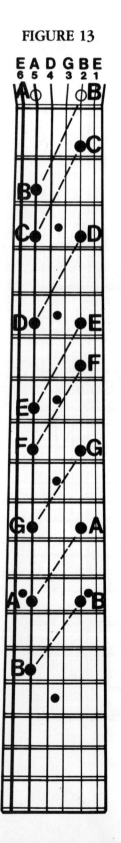

FIGURE 14

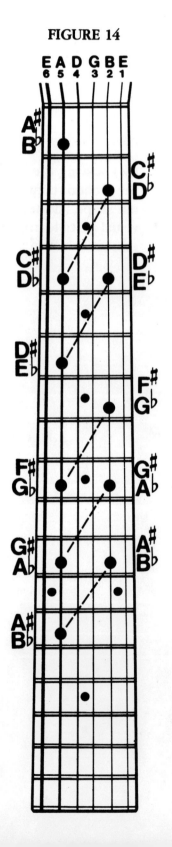

SECTION EIGHT

PLAY A DOMINANT NINTH CHORD
(ROOT ON FIFTH STRING)

FIGURE 15

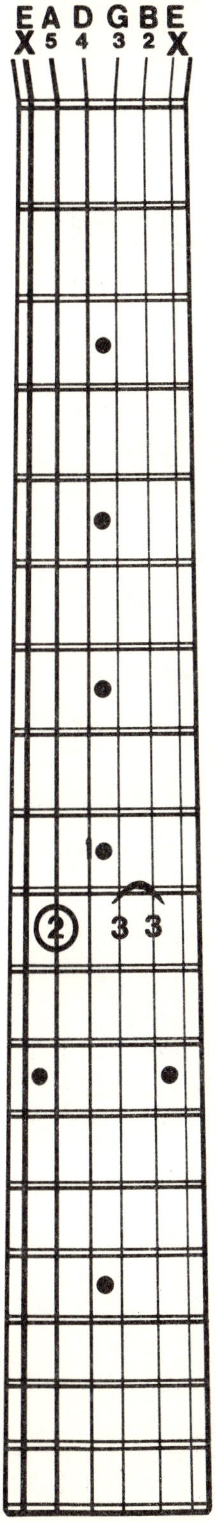

Memorize the G dominant ninth chord
shown in Fig. 15

Play the dominant ninth chord through all the keys below using the same procedure previously described. (NOTE: "G dominant ninth" is commonly abbreviated "G9").

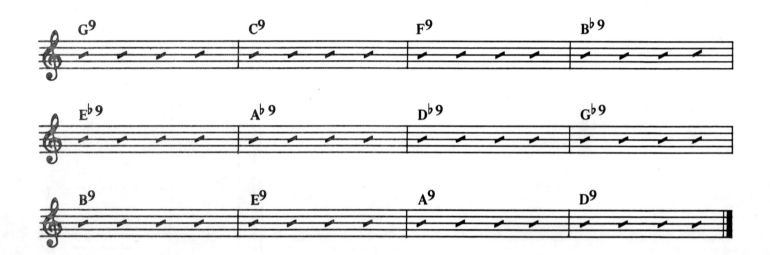

SECTION NINE

PLAY CHORDS AND MAJOR SCALES TOGETHER IN ALL KEYS

STEP 1: Pre-record the chords below on a tape recorder at a slow to moderate tempo using a metronome. Play each line twice and then go on to the next without stopping. Hold each chord for four beats on the metronome (as indicated by the slash marks on the staff).
*Remember you're going to have to play the scales later so don't record the chords too fast.

STEP 2: Play back the recorded chord changes and play the indicated scales ("Key of C" etc.) along with the recording. You may play the notes of the scale in any order. The scale does not have to start on the tonic to maintain its characteristic sound; a Bb scale sounds like a Bb scale no matter what note you start on. Move from one key to the next without breaking tempo. Mistake-proof your practice by using a metronome setting slow enough to eliminate any possibility of error. Remember: hold each note as long as possible to attain speed and smoothness of execution. Make no mistake more than once.

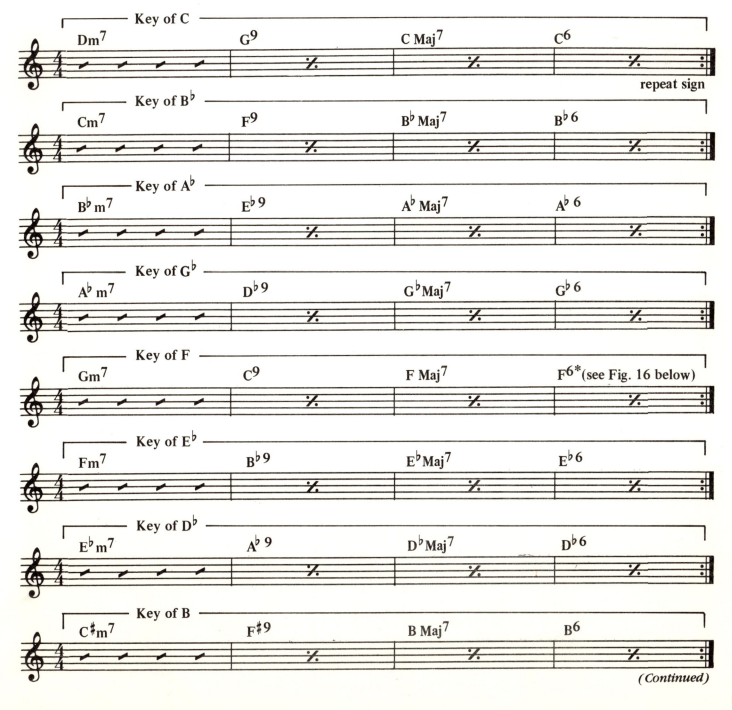

(Continued)

Fig. 16 shows the F6 chord in open fingering. Memorize the alterations in fingering created by the open string.

FIGURE 16

SECTION TEN

PLAY A TUNE

STEP 1: Pre-record the typical chord progression shown below several times without stopping. Use the chord forms just learned. Play at a mistake-proof tempo, hold each note as long as possible.
*Remember you're going to have to play the scales later so don't record the chords too fast.

STEP 2: Play back the recorded changes and play the indicated scales along with the recording. Play the notes of the scale in any order; change from one key to the next without breaking tempo.

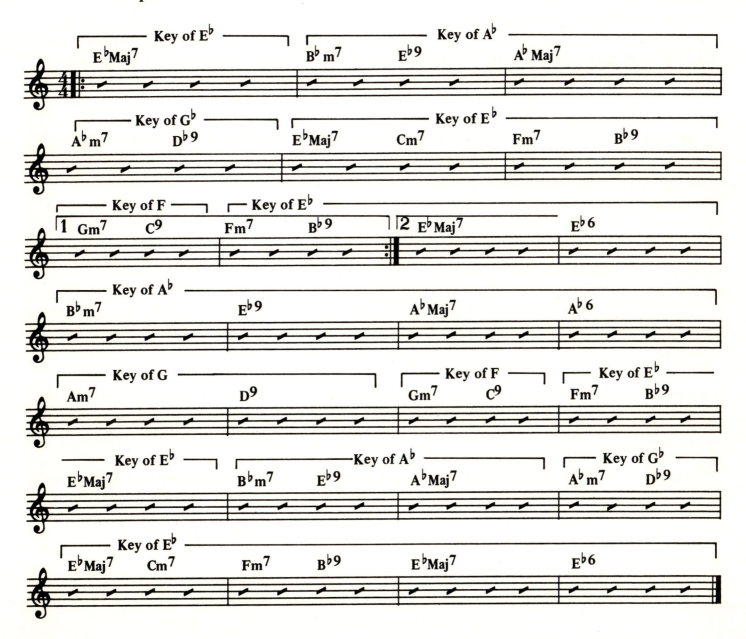

NOTE: The chords are played in this order:
From the beginning, go as far as the repeat sign at the end of the first ending (the first ending is marked by a small "1" above the bar at the beginning of the third line). Then go back to the beginning (where there is another repeat sign) and play the first two lines again, this time taking the second ending (marked by a "2") instead of the first and continuing to the end of the tune.

DO NOT BREAK TEMPO BETWEEN SECTIONS

CHAPTER ONE-END TEST

This series of questions is designed to test your knowledge of the information contained in this chapter. There is a time limit on the completion of each question - *do not* go beyond that limit. Use a clock or timer to insure accuracy; if you do not complete the question in the time allotted, stop and go on to the next question. When you are finished, go back and check your answers against the information contained in each section. If you missed any questions, were unable to complete any questions in the time allotted, or were generally hazy about any of the information, go back to the specific section in which you had trouble and review. Then take the test again (just the questions you missed). DO NOT GO TO THE NEXT CHAPTER until you can complete the test perfectly in the time allotted. Remember: review only the information you're *not* sure of; don't waste time going back over things you already know.

NOTE: The overall time limit at the end of the test includes enough extra time to set up the tape recorder, resharpen pencil, take a brief pause between questions, etc. Before you begin the test, get all of the necessary materials handy so that you have the maximum amount of actual work time. The entire test must be completed within the overall amount of time allowed. If you finish early, use any extra time to go back and check your answers.

SECTION ONE

3 minutes   1) WITHOUT THE GUITAR, write the number of the fret where each of the following notes is located on the first string:

C _____ , G# _____ , Eb _____ , A _____ , D# _____ , Bb _____

3 minutes   2) WITHOUT THE GUITAR, write the number of the fret where each of the following notes is located on the fourth string:

Db _____ , G _____ , C# _____ , F _____ , Ab _____ , F# _____

SECTION TWO

5 minutes   1) WITH THE GUITAR, play the major scale fingering pattern in the following keys, ascending and descending, one note per beat of the metronome, no mistakes. Allow four beats of the metronome between keys; do not break tempo.

Ab, B, E, C, F, G#, Db

SECTION THREE

3 minutes   1) WITHOUT THE GUITAR, write the number of the fret where each of the following notes is located on the sixth string:

B _____ , F# _____ , E _____ , Bb _____ , C _____ , Eb _____

SECTION FOUR

1 minute   1) WITH THE GUITAR, play the following minor seventh chords, allowing each chord to ring four beats on the metronome and moving to the next *without breaking tempo*:

Gm7, Ebm7, F#m7, Dm7, Am7, Em7

SECTION FIVE

1 minute   1) WITH THE GUITAR, play the following major seventh chords, four beats per chord, moving from one to the next without breaking tempo:

Fmaj7, Bmaj7, Abmaj7, Dmaj7, Gmaj7, Emaj7

SECTION SIX

1 minute   1) WITH THE GUITAR, play the following major sixth chords, four beats per chord, changing from one to the next without breaking tempo:

C6, Gb6, Bb6, Eb6, F6, Db6

SECTION SEVEN

3 minutes 1) WITHOUT THE GUITAR, write the number of the fret where each of the following notes is located on the second string:

E _____ , A# _____ , B _____ , Gb _____ , A _____ , Eb _____

3 minutes 2) WITHOUT THE GUITAR, write the number of the fret where each of the following notes is located on the fifth string:

G _____ , C# _____ , B _____ , Eb _____ , G# _____ , F _____

SECTION EIGHT

1 minute 1) WITH THE GUITAR, play the following dominant ninth chords, four beats per chord, changing from one to the next without breaking tempo:

G9, Db9, F9, Ab9, C9, Bb9

SECTION NINE

10 minutes 1) WITH THE GUITAR, follow the instructions given for Section Nine (page 21) and record the chords, play them back, and play the major scales for the following keys (without breaking tempo between keys):

Bb, F, C, G, D, A

OVERALL TIME LIMIT
45 MINUTES

Chapter Two

INSTRUCTION TWO: Go to the test at the end of Chapter Two (page 47). If you can complete the test *without mistakes, within the time limit* (35 minutes), you may go immediately to Instruction Three on page 48. If you cannot complete the test as prescribed, go back to the first page of Chapter Two (page 27) and continue your study of the book there. Memorize the scale pattern and chord forms and play them in your head when walking, taking a shower, waiting in line, etc. Remember: speed is the byproduct of accuracy. *Do not* go to Chapter Three until you can complete the test at the end of Chapter Two comfortably within the time limit (35 minutes).

SECTION ONE

PLAY ANOTHER MAJOR SCALE PATTERN

Memorize the major scale fingering pattern for the key of F as shown in Fig. 17 below. This is another way of playing the same major scale learned in Chapter One—notice that the tonics (circled) are on the fifth and second strings.

In order to play this major scale pattern in any other key, simply locate the tonic on the fifth and/or second strings and play the same fingering. Fig 18 shows the same pattern in the key of C, using open strings. Memorize the differences in fingering.

FIGURE 17

MAJOR SCALE FINGERING PATTERN
KEY OF F

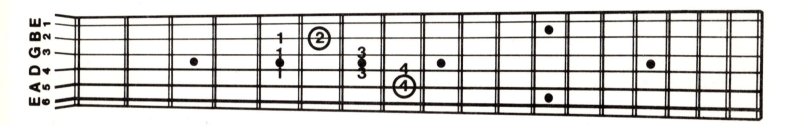

FIGURE 18

MAJOR SCALE FINGERING PATTERN
KEY OF C

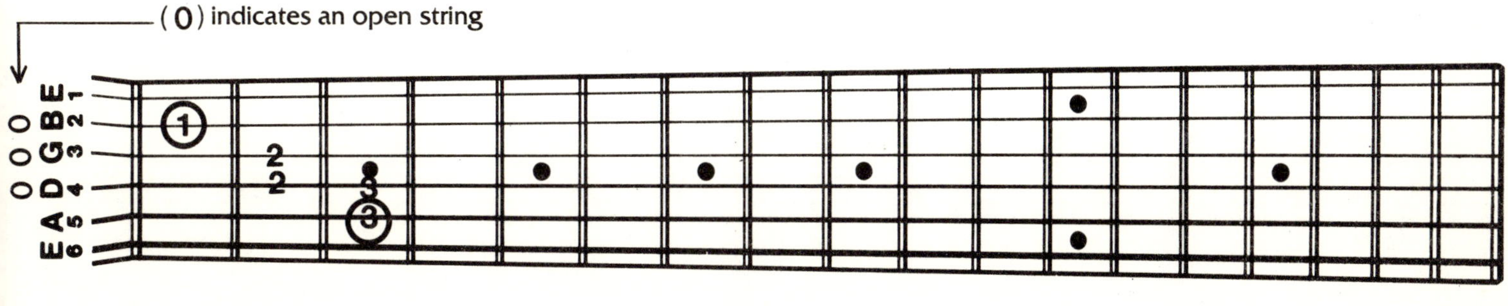

— (O) indicates an open string

Using the major scale fingering pattern from Fig. 17, play the major scale in each of the keys below (memorize their locations on the fingerboard so you can locate them quickly). Using a metronome, play the scales ascending and descending, one note per beat. Use a slow enough setting to mistake-proof your practice. Hold each note as long as possible—remember: SPEED IS THE BYPRODUCT OF ACCURACY.

SECTION TWO

PLAY A MINOR SEVENTH CHORD
(ROOT ON FIFTH STRING)

Memorize the G minor seventh chord shown in Fig. 19.

Note that the root of the chord (G) is on the fifth string (circled).

To play an E minor seventh chord, simply play the same shape with root on the fifth string, seventh fret.

NOTE: If this chord form is too difficult at this time, eliminate the root (lowest note) and just play the top three notes.

Keep the position of the root in mind and add it as soon as possible.

By using the full chord, you will develop a longer reach.

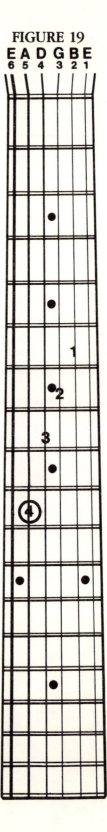

FIGURE 19

Play the minor seventh chord through all the keys below, holding each chord for four beats on the metronome. Move from one chord to the next quickly and cleanly, holding each one as long as possible.

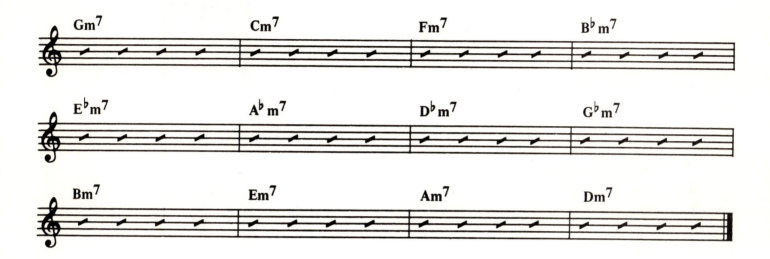

SECTION THREE

PLAY A MAJOR SEVENTH CHORD
(ROOT ON FIFTH STRING)

Memorize the F major seventh chord shown in Fig. 20.

Note that the root is on the fifth string.

FIGURE 20

Play the major seventh chord through all the keys below using the same procedure as for the minor seventh chord.

F Maj⁷   B♭ Maj⁷   E♭ Maj⁷   A♭ Maj⁷

D♭ Maj⁷   G♭ Maj⁷   B Maj⁷   E Maj⁷

A Maj⁷   D Maj⁷   G Maj⁷   C Maj⁷

FIGURE 21

This is the same chord shown in figure 20 but in open position. Memorize the fingering alterations created by the open strings.

SECTION FOUR

PLAY A MAJOR SIXTH CHORD
(ROOT ON FIFTH STRING)

FIGURE 22

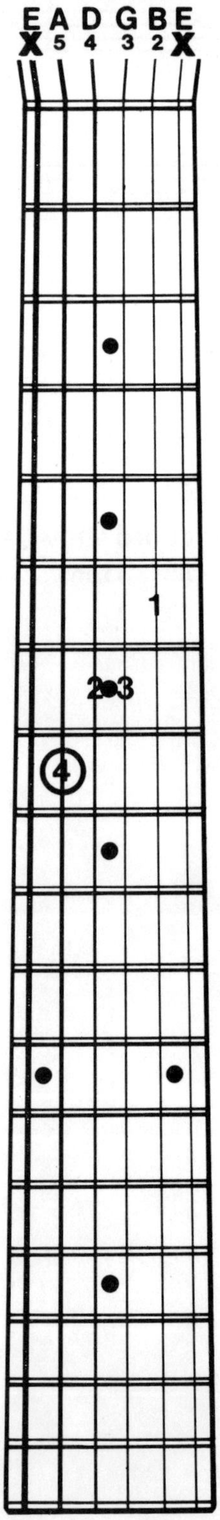

Memorize the F major sixth chord
shown in Fig. 22.

Play the major sixth chord through all the keys below.

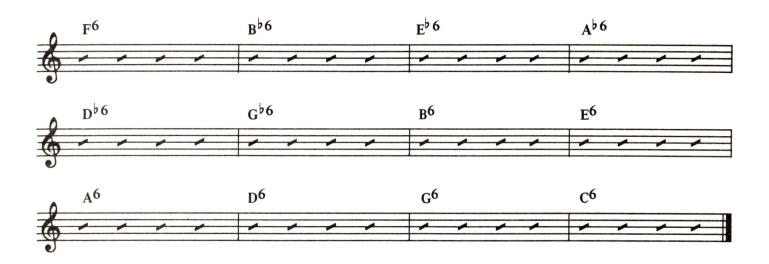

SECTION FIVE

PLAY A DOMINANT NINTH CHORD
(ROOT ON SIXTH STRING)

Memorize the C dominant ninth chord shown in Fig. 23.

Note that the root is on the sixth string.

This chord form will also help develop your reach.

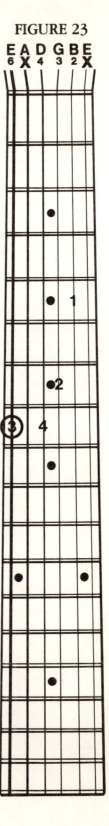

FIGURE 23

Play the dominant ninth chord through all the keys below using the same procedure previously described.

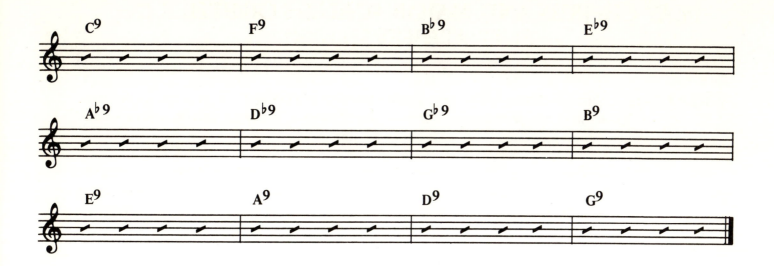

C^9 F^9 $B^\flat 9$ $E^\flat 9$

$A^\flat 9$ $D^\flat 9$ $G^\flat 9$ B^9

E^9 A^9 D^9 G^9

FIGURE 24

This is the same chord shown in Fig. 23 but in open position. Memorize the fingering alterations created by the open string.

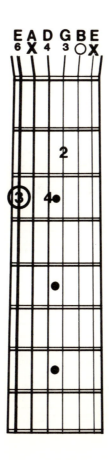

SECTION SIX

PLAY CHORDS AND MAJOR SCALES TOGETHER IN ALL KEYS

STEP 1: Pre-record the chords below (using forms learned in Sections 2-5) on a tape recorder at a slow to moderate tempo using a metronome. Play each line twice and then go on to the next without stopping. Hold each chord for four beats.
*Remember you're going to have to play the scales later so don't record the chords too fast.

STEP 2: Play back the recorded chord changes and play the scales for the keys indicated using the major scale pattern shown in Section 1. Play the notes of the scale in any order. Move from one key to the next without breaking tempo. Use a setting slow enough to be mistake-proof.

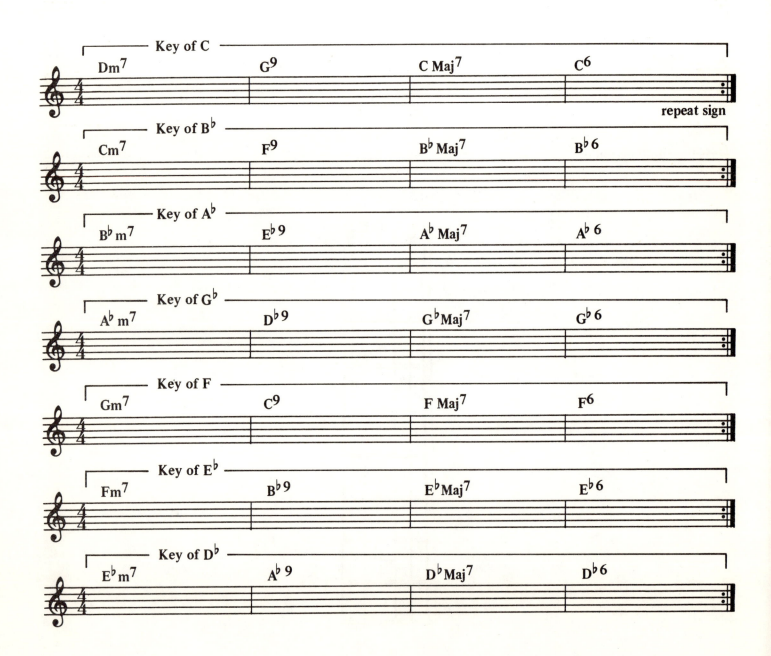

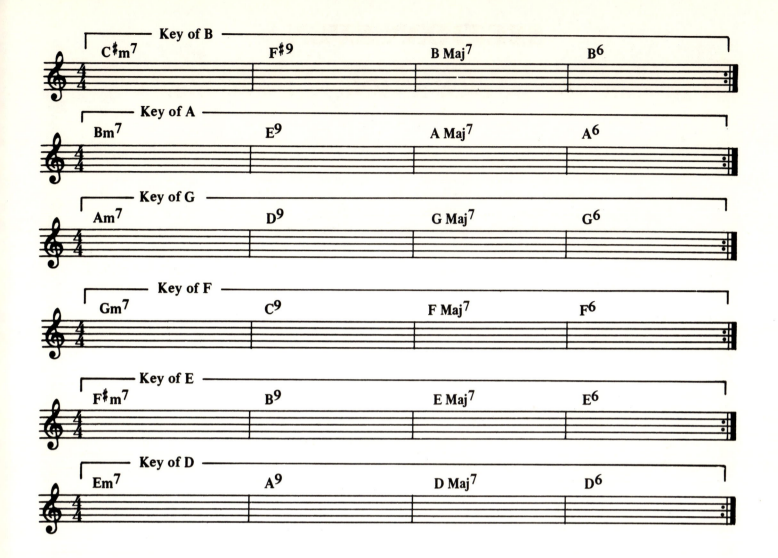

SECTION SEVEN

PLAY A TUNE

STEP 1: Pre-record the typical chord progression shown below several times without stopping. Use the chord forms just learned.

*Remember you're going to have to play the scales later so don't record the chords too fast.

STEP 2: Play back the recorded changes and play the indicated scales along with the recording (using only the major scale form learned in Section 1). Play the notes of the scale in any order; change from one key to the next without breaking tempo. Hold each note as long as possible.

SECTION EIGHT

COMBINE THE CHORDS AND MAJOR SCALE FORMS

STEP 1: Pre-record each line below twice, playing the first time through using the first set of minor, dominant, and major chords learned (Chapter One) and the second time with the second set of chords learned (Chapter Two). DO NOT STOP between chord sets or between keys—use a metronome setting slow enough to be mistake-proof.
*Remember you're going to have to play the scales later so don't record the chords too fast.

STEP 2: Play back the recorded changes and play the scales for the keys indicated using the pattern learned in Chapter 1 the first time through and the pattern learned in Chapter 2 the second time through. Move from one pattern to the next and one key to the next *without breaking tempo*.

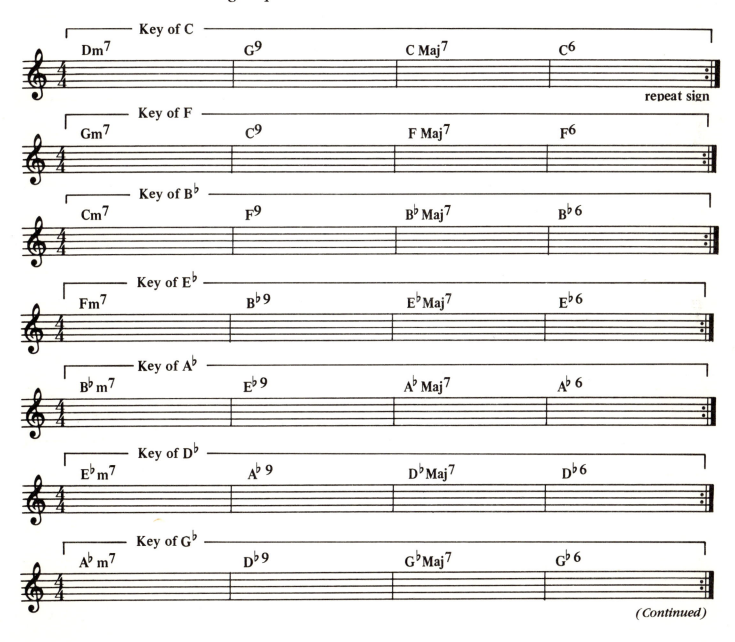

(Continued)

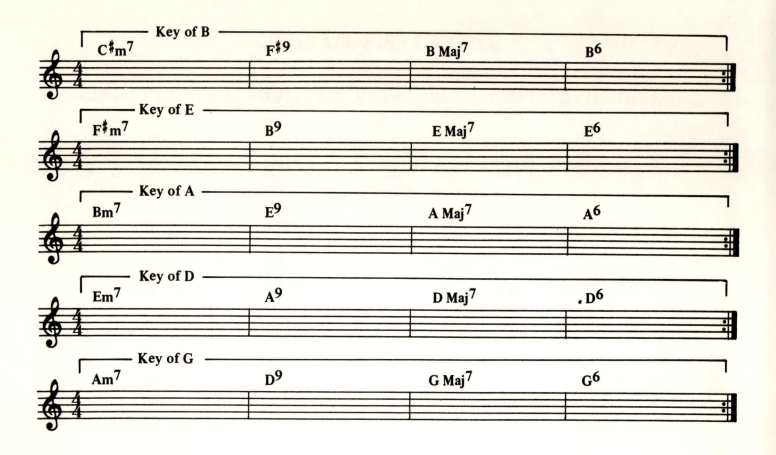

COMBINE THE CHORDS AND MAJOR SCALE FORMS *(Continued)*

STEP 1: Pre-record the following chord changes, playing each line once. Alternate sets of chord forms from line to line: play the chord forms from Chapter One for the first line, the chord forms from Chapter Two for the second line, from Chapter One for the third line, from Chapter Two for the fourth line, etc. The appropriate chapter number is indicated to the left of each line. See Figs. 25-28 below for an example of how the successive sets of chords and scales will follow each other on the fingerboard.

STEP 2: Play back the changes and play the major scales for the keys indicated, alternate patterns from line to line just as you did for the chords. Once again, refer to Figs. 25-28 for an example of how the scale forms will follow each other on the fingerboard.

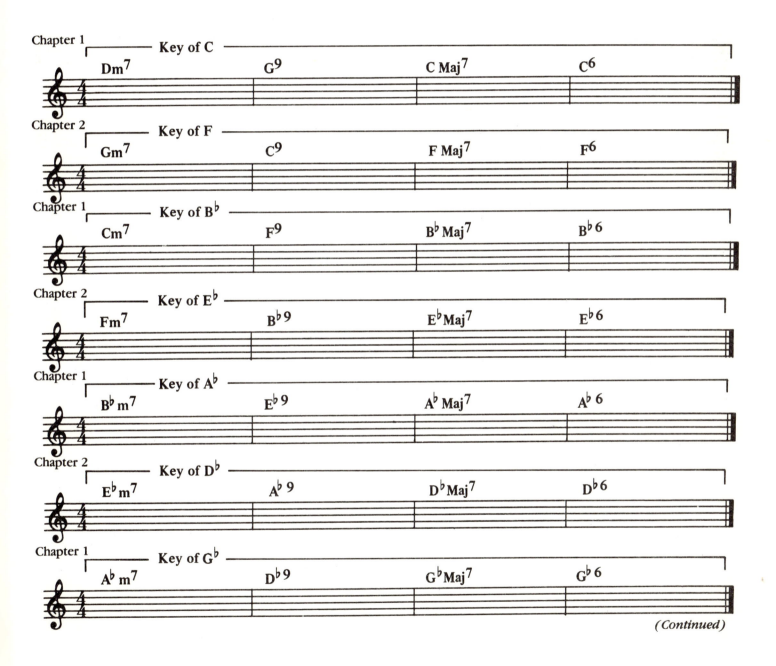

(Continued)

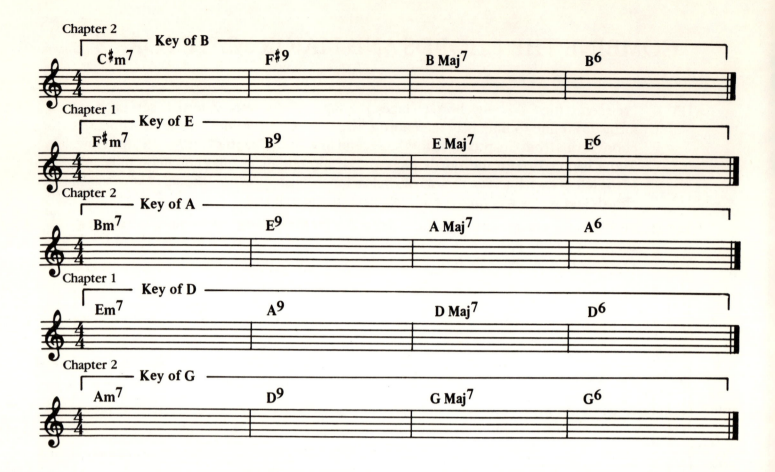

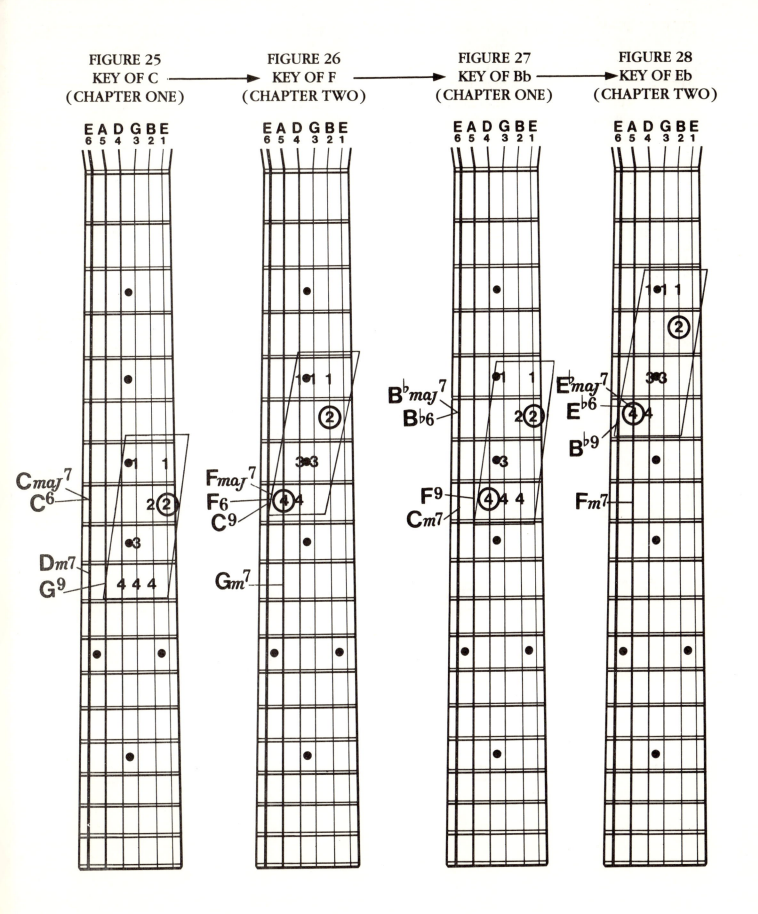

FIGURE 25
KEY OF C
(CHAPTER ONE)

FIGURE 26
KEY OF F
(CHAPTER TWO)

FIGURE 27
KEY OF Bb
(CHAPTER ONE)

FIGURE 28
KEY OF Eb
(CHAPTER TWO)

Lines from chord symbols point to roots of the indicated chords.

PLAY A TUNE USING COMBINED CHORD AND SCALE FORMS

STEP 1: Pre-record the progression below (the same one used previously) using *any* of the chord forms learned so far in any combination. Some combinations will obviously be more practical than others, but feel free to experiment.

STEP 2: Play back the recorded changes and play the scales for the keys indicated along with the recording. use either major scale'pattern learned so far - switch from one to the other where convenient, but do not break tempo. Play the notes in any order, hold each note as long as possible.

CHAPTER TWO-END TEST

Review the instructions at the beginning of the test for Chapter One. REMEMBER: DO NOT GO ON TO THE NEXT CHAPTER until you can complete the test perfectly in the time allotted. Review *only* the information you're not sure of, don't waste time going back over things you already know.

NOTE: Check the overall time limit at the end of the test.

SECTION ONE

5 minutes

1) WITH THE GUITAR, play the major scale fingering pattern in the following keys, ascending and descending, one note per beat of the metronome, no mistakes. Rest for four beats of the metronome between keys, *do not* break tempo:

A, C, F, Db, Gb, Ab, C#

SECTION TWO

1 minute

1) WITH THE GUITAR, play the following minor seventh chords, allowing each chord to ring for four beats on the metronome and moving to the next chord *without breaking tempo*:

F#m7, Dm7, Fm7, Dbm7, Abm7, Ebm7

SECTION THREE

1 minute

1) WITH THE GUITAR, play the following major seventh chords, four beats per chord, moving from one to the next without breaking tempo:

Gbmaj7, Cmaj7, Bmaj7, Ebmaj7, Abmaj7, Fmaj7

SECTION FOUR

1 minute

1) WITH THE GUITAR, play the following major sixth chords, four beats per chord, moving from one to the next without breaking tempo:·

D6, Ab6, C6, F6, G6, Eb6

SECTION FIVE

1 minute

1) WITH THE GUITAR, play the following dominant ninth chords, four beats per chord, moving from one to the next without breaking tempo:

F9, Eb9, Bb9, C9, Gb9, E9

SECTION SIX

10 minutes

1) WITH THE GUITAR, follow the instructions given for Section Six (page 38) and record the chords, play them back, and play the major scales for the following keys without breaking tempo between keys:

E, B, Gb, Db, Ab, Eb

SECTION EIGHT

10 minutes

1) WITH THE GUITAR, follow the instructions for the exercise which alternates chord and scale forms from line to line (page 43) and play the chords and scales for the following keys without breaking tempo:

Db, Gb, B, E, A, D

OVERALL TIME LIMIT
35 MINUTES

Chapter Three

INSTRUCTION THREE:

Go to the test at the end of Chapter Three (page 63). If you can complete the test *without mistakes, within the time limit* (27 minutes), you may go immediately to Instruction Four on page 64. If you cannot complete the test as prescribed, go back to the first page of Chapter Three (page 49) and continue your study of the book there. Commit the scale and chord forms totally to memory until they are just as much second nature as using a knife and fork. Do not go to Chapter Four until you can complete the test at the end of Chapter Three comfortably within the time limit (27 minutes).

SECTION ONE

PLAY THE NATURAL MINOR SCALE IN ALL KEYS

So far we have looked only at major scales and major keys; in this chapter and the next we will learn some fingerings for the minor scales and their related chords.

If we take the C major scale fingering pattern learned in Chapter One and extend it by adding two notes below the tonic on the fourth string, we now have a C major scale starting on the note A. If we play the scale as far as the A on the second string, we have played an A natural minor scale (see Fig. 29). In other words, the A natural minor scale, has the same fingering as the C major scale but the tonic is the note A rather than the note C.

FIGURE 29

◯ = Tonic Of The A Minor Scale

⬭ = Tonic Of The C Major Scale

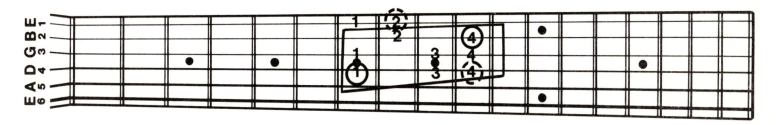

Memorize the minor scale fingering pattern for the key of A minor as shown in Fig. 30. The tonic tones (the "A's") are circled. In order to play this minor scale in any other key, simply locate the tonic on the fourth and/or second strings and play the same pattern.

FIGURE 30

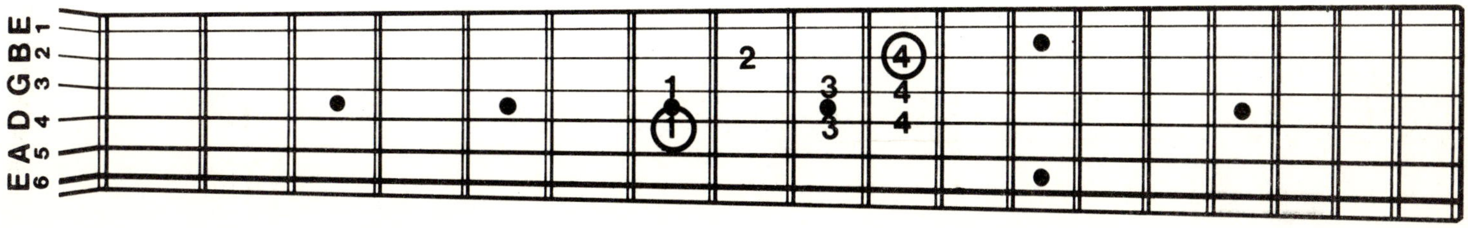

Using the minor scale fingering pattern from Fig. 30, play the minor scale in each of the keys below (memorize their locations on the fingerboard so you can find them quickly). Using a metronome, play the scales ascending and descending, one note per beat. Move from key to key without interrupting the rhythm.

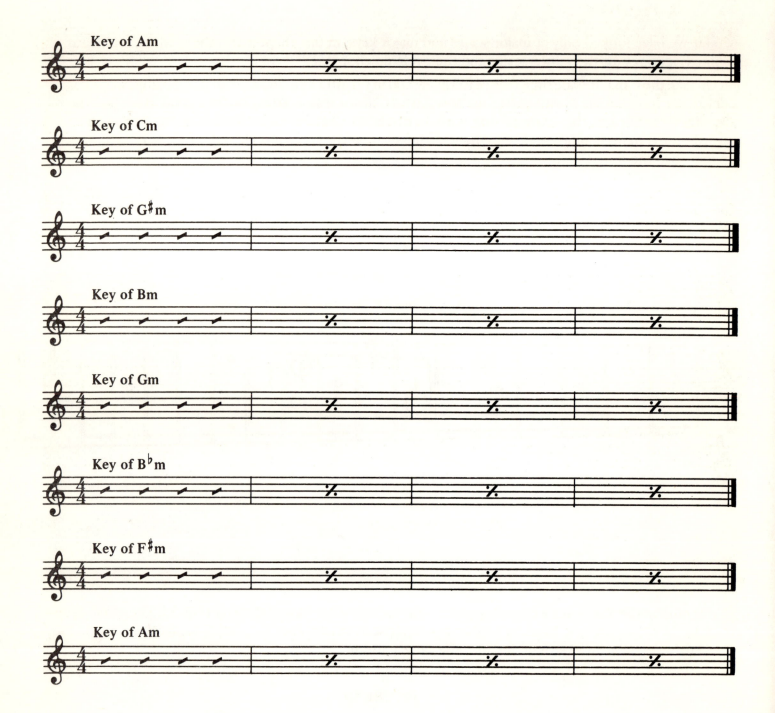

SECTION TWO

PLAY THE HARMONIC MINOR SCALE IN ALL KEYS

The most commonly applied minor scale is called the harmonic minor scale. It is exactly the same as the natural minor scale with the exception of one note. We simply raise the next-to-highest note in the natural minor scale (in the key of A minor, the note G) by one fret (to G#). The resulting scale is the harmonic minor scale, with the fingering shown in Fig. 31 below.

Memorize the fingering pattern shown for the key of A harmonic minor. Note that there is only one note different from A natural minor, so there is only one new note to remember.

FIGURE 31

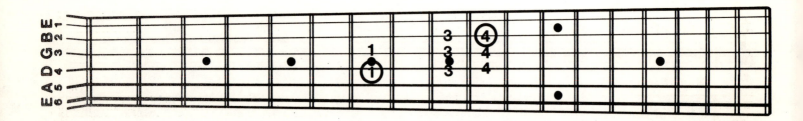

Using the harmonic minor scale fingering pattern from Fig. 31, play the harmonic minor scale in each of the keys below (memorize their locations on the fingerboard). Using a metronome, play the scales ascending and descending, one note per beat. Use a metronome setting slow enough to be mistake-proof; allow no string buzzes or "dead" notes. SPEED IS A BYPRODUCT OF ACCURACY. Shift scales without interrupting the rhythm.

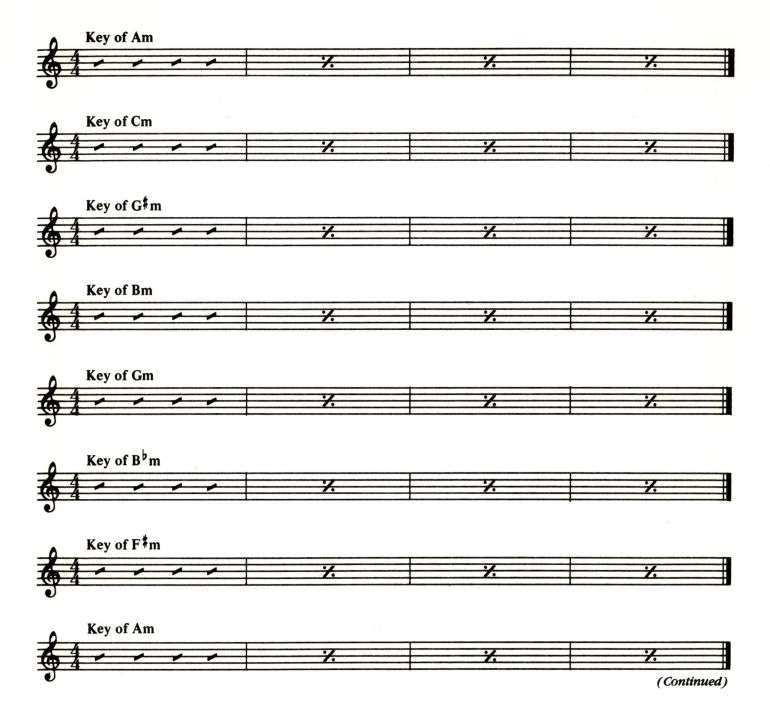

(Continued)

SECTION THREE

PLAY A MINOR SEVEN FLAT FIVE CHORD
(ROOT ON SIXTH STRING)

Memorize the B minor seven flat five chord shown in Fig. 32.

To play an Eb minor seven flat five chord, play the same shape with the root on the sixth string, eleventh fret.

(Note: "minor seven flat five" is often abbreviated "m7(b5)").

FIGURE 32

Play the minor seven flat five chord through all the keys below, holding each chord for four beats on the metronome. Move from one chord to the next quickly and cleanly, holding each one as long as possible.

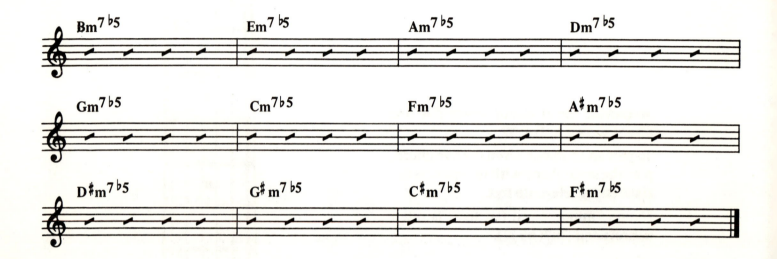

SECTION FOUR

PLAY A MINOR CHORD (ROOT ON SIXTH STRING)

Memorize the A minor chord shown in Fig. 33.

Note that there are roots on the sixth, fourth, and first strings;

Any one of these could be used to help locate the chord.

(Note: "minor" is often abbreviated simply as "m").

FIGURE 33

Play the minor chord through all the keys below, holding each chord for four beats on the metronome.

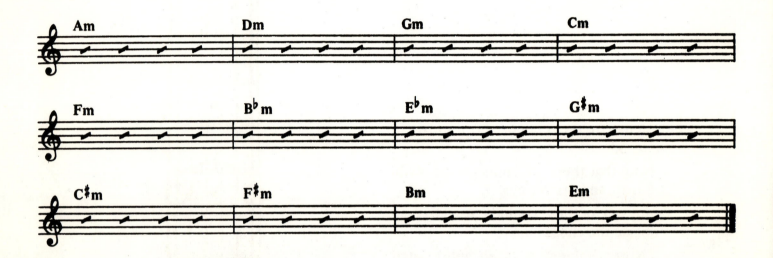

SECTION FIVE

PLAY A DOMINANT SEVENTH CHORD
(ROOT ON FIFTH STRING)

FIGURE 34

Memorize the E dominant seventh chord shown in Fig. 34.

Note that there are roots on the fifth and second strings; either of these could be used to help locate the chord.

(Note: "dominant seventh" is often abbreviated simply as "7").

Play the dominant seventh chord through all the keys below, holding each chord for four beats on the metronome.

SECTION SIX

PLAY CHORDS AND MINOR SCALES TOGETHER IN ALL KEYS

STEP 1: Pre-record the chords below on a tape recorder at a slow to moderate tempo using a metronome. Play each line two times and then go on to the next without stopping. Hold each chord for four beats on the metronome.

STEP 2: Play back the changes and play the indicated *harmonic minor* scales (Key of Am, etc.) along with the recording. Play the notes of the scale in any order. Move from one key to the next without breaking tempo. Use a setting slow enough to be mistake-proof.

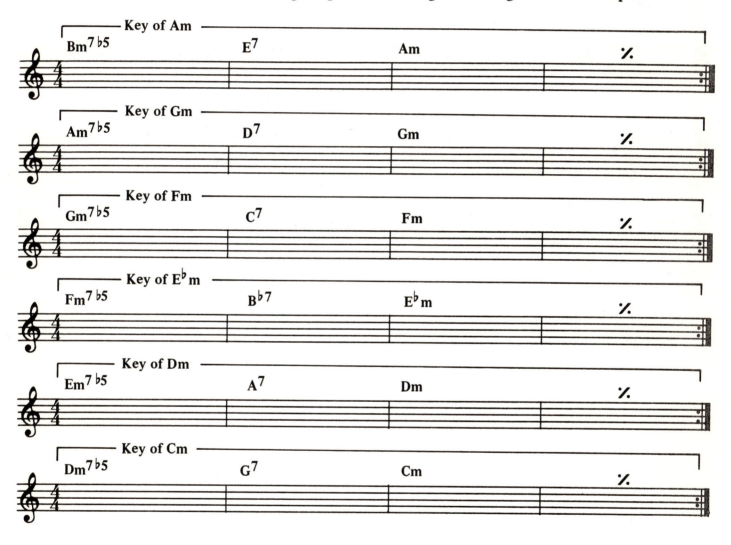

(Continued from previous page)

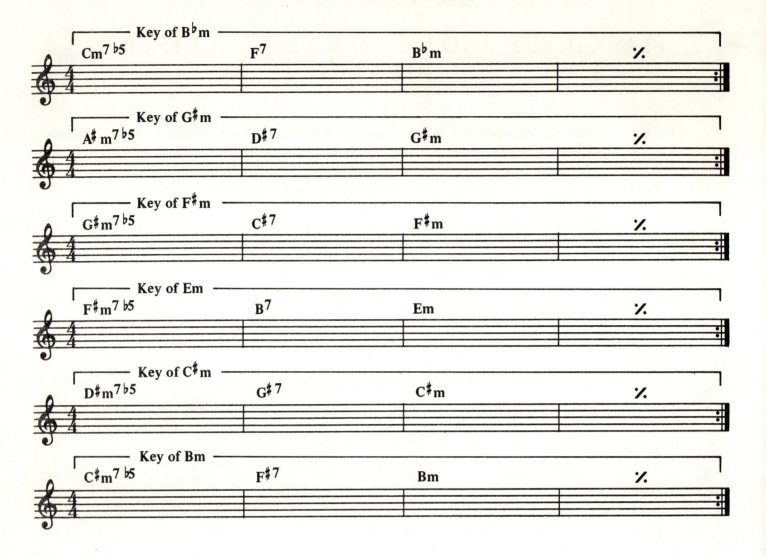

CHAPTER THREE-END TEST

Review the instructions for the test on Chapter One. Do not go on to the next chapter until you can complete the test perfectly in the time allotted. Review only the information you're not sure of. Check the overall time limit at the end of the test *before* you begin.

SECTION ONE

5 minutes   1) WITH THE GUITAR, play the natural minor scale fingering pattern in the following keys, ascending and descending, one note per beat, no mistakes. Allow four beats of the metronome between keys, do not break tempo:

Cm,   Ebm,   G#m,   Em,   Am,   Bm

SECTION TWO

5 minutes   1) WITH THE GUITAR, play the harmonic minor scale fingering pattern in the following keys, ascending and descending, one note per beat, no mistakes. Allow four beats on the metronome between keys, do not break tempo:

Fm,   G#m,   C#m,   Am,   Dm,   Em

SECTION THREE

1 minute   1) WITH THE GUITAR, play the following minor seven flat five chords, four beats per chord, moving from one to the next without breaking tempo:

G#m7b5,   Em7b5,   Gm7b5,   D#m7b5,   A#m7b5,   Fm7b5

SECTION FOUR

1 minute   1) WITH THE GUITAR, play the following minor chords, four beats per chord, moving from one to the next without breaking tempo:

G#m,   Em,   Cm,   Fm,   Gm,   C#m

SECTION FIVE

1 minute   1) WITH THE GUITAR, play the following dominant seventh chords, four beats per chord, moving from one to the next without breaking tempo:

E7,   C7,   G#7,   D7,   Bb7,   F#7

SECTION SIX

10 minutes   1) WITH THE GUITAR, follow the instructions given for Section Six (page 61) and record the chords, play them back, and play the harmonic minor scales for the following keys without breaking tempo between keys:

Am,   Fm,   Dm,   Gm,   Ebm,   Cm

OVERALL TIME LIMIT
27 MINUTES

Chapter Four

INSTRUCTION FOUR:

Go to the test at the end of Chapter Four (page 86). If you can complete the test comfortably without mistakes, within the time limit (65 minutes), go immediately to Instruction Five on page 88. If you cannot complete the test as prescribed, go to the first page of Chapter Four (page 65) and continue your study of the book there. The tune at the end of the chapter must be played just as accurately as the scale form at the beginning of the chapter; how long it takes to get from the beginning to the end is unimportant. *Do not* go to Chapter Five until you can complete the test at the end of Chapter Four comfortably within the time limit (65 minutes).

SECTION ONE

KNOW THE NAMES OF THE NOTES ON THE THIRD STRING

Referring to the figures shown below, memorize the names of all of the notes on the third string. This will be easy because the names are identical to the notes on the fifth string, two frets down, as shown by the dotted line. Also note the relationship to the second string.

FIGURE 35

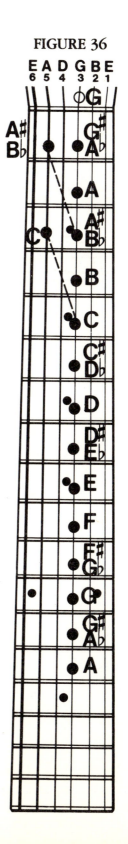

FIGURE 36

SECTION TWO

ANOTHER FINGERING FOR THE NATURAL MINOR SCALE

Memorize the minor scale fingering pattern for the key of D minor as shown in Fig. 37. Note the similarity to the major scale fingering shown in Chapter Two - the notes in both scales are the same, but the natural minor starts on D rather than F, so D is the tonic. In order to play this scale in any other key, simply locate the tonic on the fifth and/or third strings and play the same pattern.

FIGURE 37

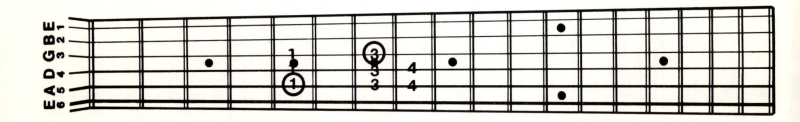

Using the minor scale fingering pattern from Fig. 37, play the minor scale in each of the keys below (memorize their locations on the fingerboard so you can find them quickly). Using a metronome, play the scales ascending and descending, one note per beat. Move from key to key without interrupting the rhythm.

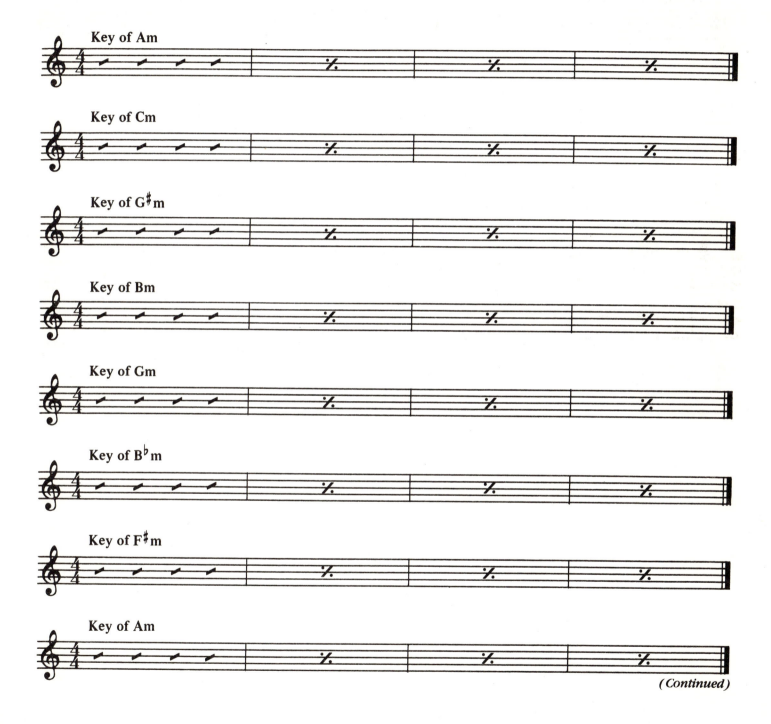

(Continued)

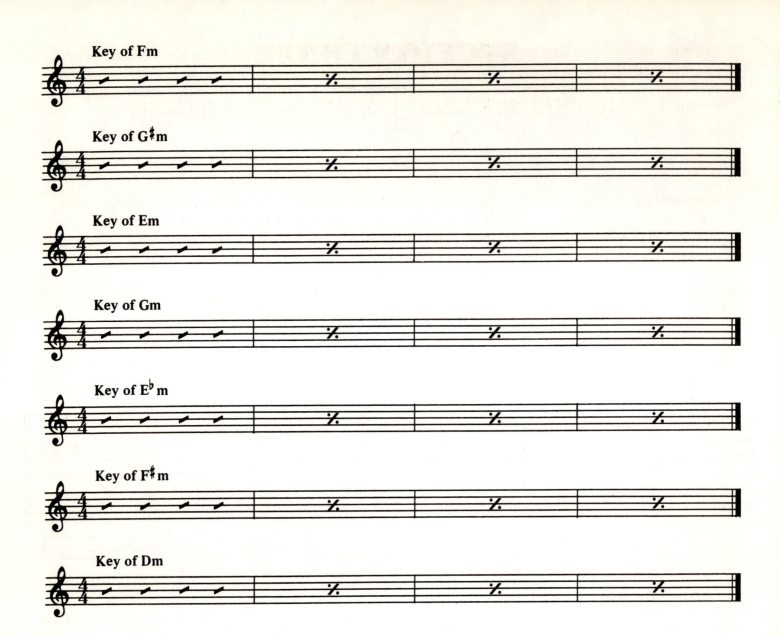

SECTION THREE

ANOTHER FINGERING FOR THE HARMONIC MINOR SCALE

Memorize the fingering pattern shown in Fig. 38 for the D harmonic minor scale. This is the same as the D natural minor scale (Fig. 37) with the exception of one note—C is raised one fret to C#. To play this scale in other keys, simply find the tonic on the fifth and/or third strings and play the same pattern.

FIGURE 38

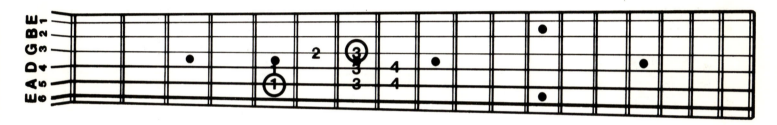

Using the harmonic minor scale fingering pattern from Fig. 38, play the minor scale in each of the keys below (memorize their locations on the fingerboard so you can find them quickly). Using a metronome, play the scales ascending and descending, one note per beat. Use a tempo slow enough to be mistake-proof. Move from key to key without interrupting the rhythm.

(Continued)

SECTION FOUR

PLAY A MINOR SEVEN FLAT FIVE CHORD
(ROOT ON FIFTH STRING)

FIGURE 39

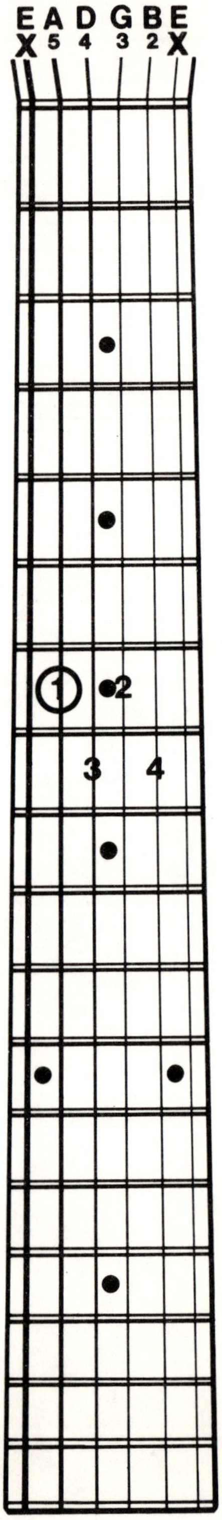

Memorize the E minor seven flat five chord shown in Fig. 39.

To play any other minor seven flat five chord, find the root on the fifth string and play the same shape.

Play the minor seven flat five chord shown in Fig. 39 through all the keys below, holding each chord for four beats on the metronome. Move from one chord to the next quickly and cleanly, holding each one as long as possible.

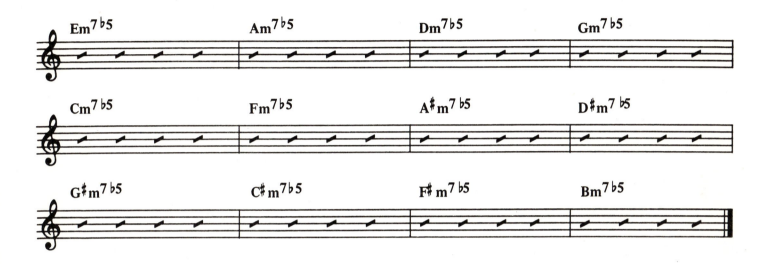

SECTION FIVE

PLAY A MINOR CHORD (ROOT ON FIFTH STRING)

FIGURE 40

Memorize the D minor chord shown in Fig. 40.

Note that there are roots on the fifth and third strings; either of these could be used to help locate the chord.

Play the minor chord shown in Fig. 40 through all the keys below, holding each chord for four beats on the metronome.

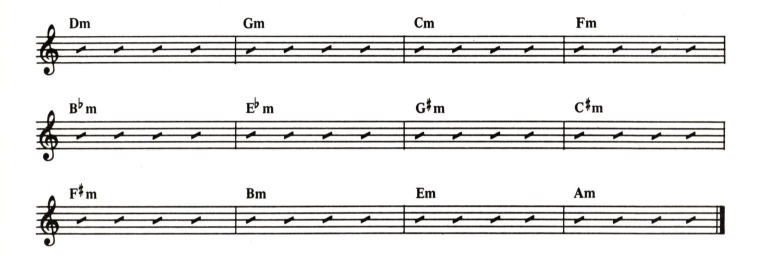

PLAY A DOMINANT SEVENTH CHORD
(ROOT ON SIXTH STRING)

FIGURE 41

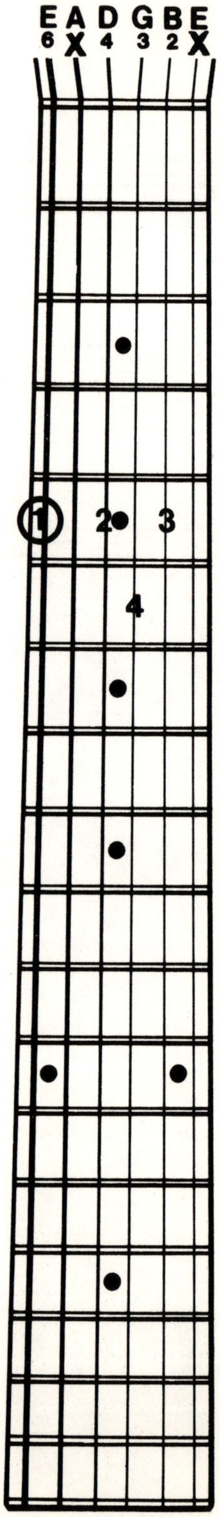

Memorize the A dominant seventh chord shown in Fig. 41.

The same shape may be used for any key; just locate the root on the sixth string.

Play the dominant chord shown in Fig. 41 through all the keys below, holding each chord for four beats on the metronome.

SECTION SEVEN

PLAY CHORDS AND MINOR SCALES TOGETHER IN ALL KEYS

STEP 1: Pre-record the chords below (from Figs. 39-41) on a tape recorder at a slow to moderate tempo using a metronome. Play each line twice and then go on the to next without stopping. Hold each chord for four beats on the metronome. Use a setting slow enough to be mistake-proof.

STEP 2: Play back the changes and play the indicated *harmonic minor* scales along with the recording. Play the notes of the scale in any order. Move from one key to the next without breaking tempo. (Note: use *only* the scale form shown in Fig. 37).

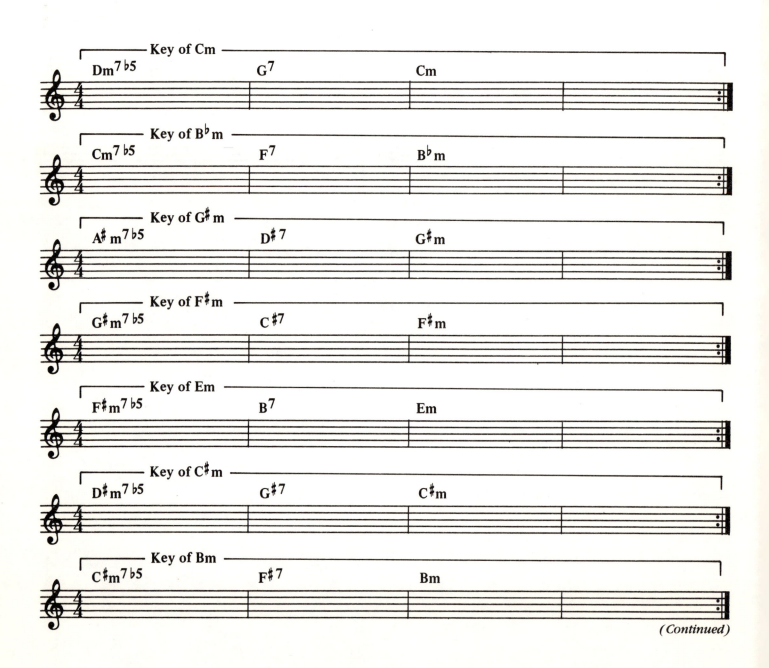

(Continued)

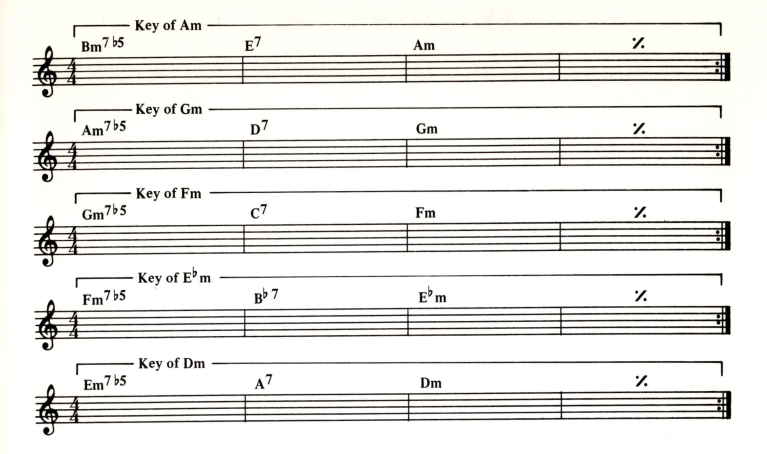

SECTION EIGHT

COMBINE THE CHORDS AND MINOR SCALE FORMS

STEP 1: Pre-record each line below twice, playing the first time through using the minor seven flat five, dominant 7, and minor chord forms learned in Chapter Three, and the second time with the chord forms learned in Chapter Four. Do not stop between chord sets or between keys - use a metronome setting slow enough to be mistake-proof.

STEP 2: Play back the recorded changes and play the scales for the keys indicated using the pattern from Chapter Three the first time and the pattern from Chapter Four the second time. Move from one pattern to the next and one key to the next *without breaking tempo*.

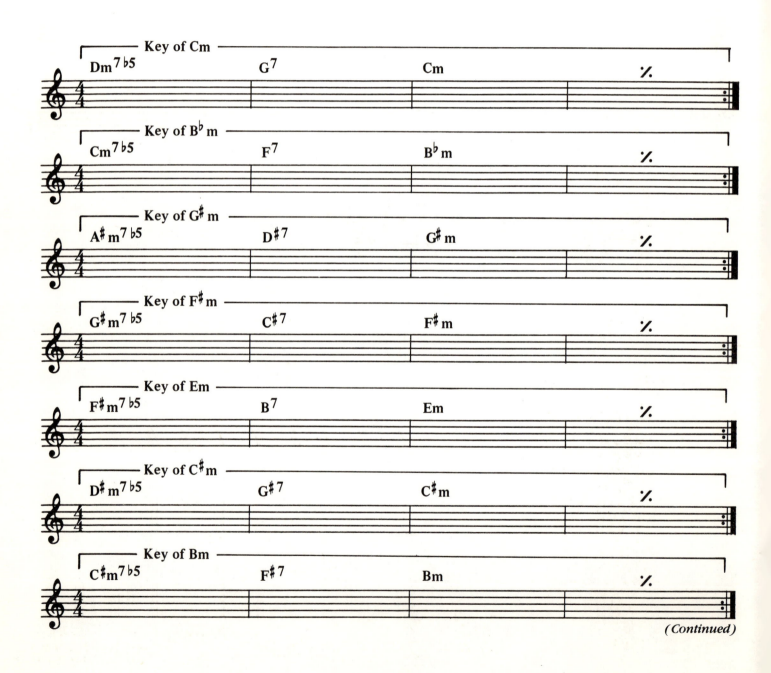

(Continued)

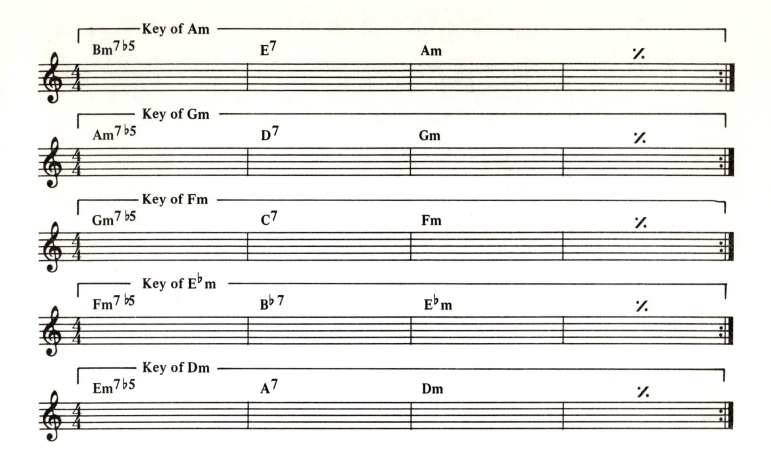

COMBINE THE CHORDS AND MAJOR SCALES FORMS *(Continued)*

STEP 1:   Pre-record the following chord changes, playing each line once. Alternate sets of chord forms from line to line: play the forms from Chapter Three for the first line, the forms from Chapter Four for the second line, the forms from Chapter Three for the third line, Chapter Four for the fourth line, etc. The appropriate chapter number is indicated to the left of each line.

Refer to Figs. 42-45 below for an example of how chords and scales will follow each other on the fingerboard in minor keys.

STEP 2:   Play back the changes and play the minor scales for the keys indicated, alternating patterns from line to line (first Chap. Three, then Chap. Four, etc.) just as you did for the chords.

(Continued)

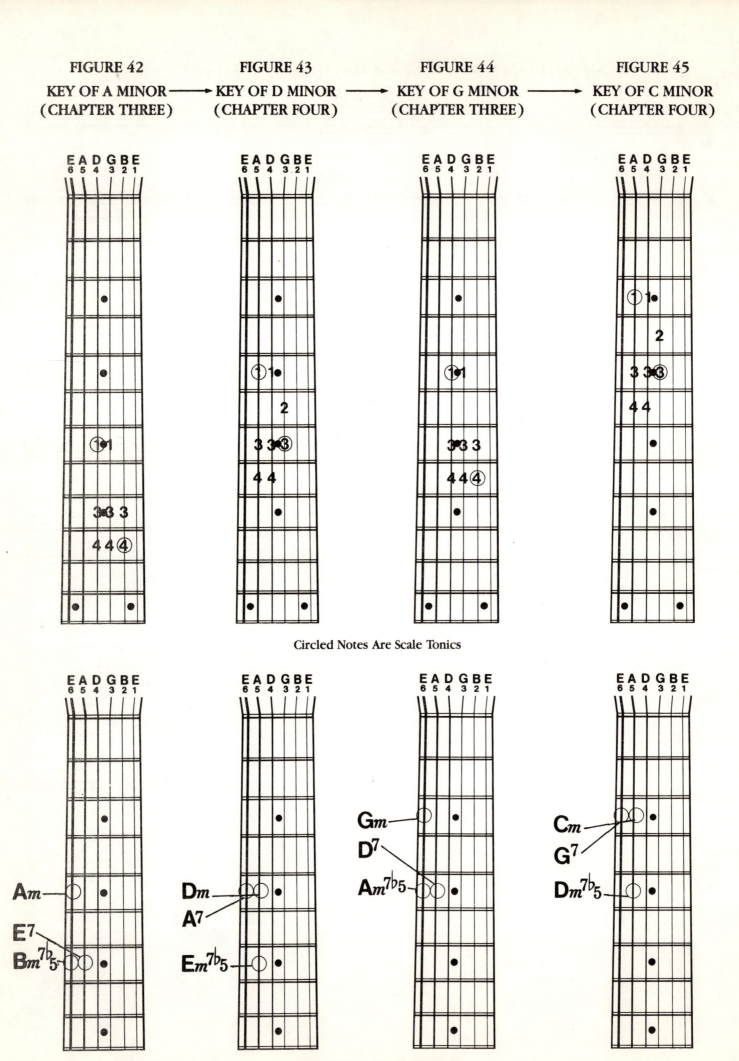

FIGURE 42
KEY OF A MINOR
(CHAPTER THREE)

FIGURE 43
KEY OF D MINOR
(CHAPTER FOUR)

FIGURE 44
KEY OF G MINOR
(CHAPTER THREE)

FIGURE 45
KEY OF C MINOR
(CHAPTER FOUR)

Circled Notes Are Scale Tonics

Circled Notes Are Chord Roots

PLAY A TUNE USING COMBINED CHORD AND SCALE FORMS

STEP 1: Pr-record the progession below using any of the chord forms learned so far in any combination. Some combinations will obviously be more practical than others, but feel free to experiment. Note that there are both major and minor keys involved.

STEP 2: Play back the recorded changes and play the scales for the keys indicated along with the recording. Use any of the major or minor scale patterns learned so far (using major scales where major keys are indicated and minor scales where minor keys are indicated, of course). Switch from one pattern to another where convenient, but do not break tempo. Play the notes in any order, hold each note as long as possible.

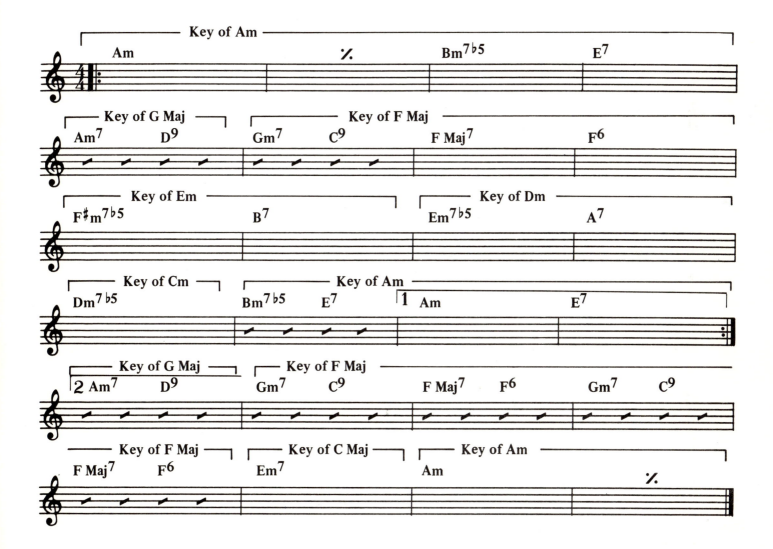

NOTE: The arrangement of this tune is the same as the one at the end of Chapter One - see that note if you need clarification.

CHAPTER FOUR-END TEST

Review the instructions for the test on Chapter One. *Do not go on to the next chapter* until you can complete the test perfectly in the time allotted. Review only the information you're not sure of, don't waste time on things you already know. Check the over all time limit at the end of the test *before* you begin.

SECTION ONE

3 minutes 1) WITHOUT THE GUITAR, write the number of the fret where each of the following notes is located on the third string:

A _____ , Db _____ , F# _____ , E _____ , Bb _____ , G _____

SECTION TWO

5 minutes 1) WITH THE GUITAR, play the natural minor scale fingering pattern in the following keys, ascending and descending, one note per beat, no mistakes. Allow four beats of the metronome between keys, do not break tempo:

C#m, Em, Am, Fm, Bbm, Cm

SECTION THREE

5 minutes 1) WITH THE GUITAR, play the harmonic minor scale fingering pattern in the following keys, ascending and descending, one note per beat, no mistakes. Allow four beats of the metronome between keys, do not break tempo:

F#m, Am, Dm, Bbm, Ebm, Fm

SECTION FOUR

1 minute 1) WITH THE GUITAR, play the following minor seven flat five chords, four beats per chord, moving from one to the next without breaking tempo:

Am7b5, Fm7b5, G#m7b5, Em7b5, Bm7b5, F#m7b5

SECTION FIVE

1 minute 1) WITH THE GUITAR, play the following minor chords, four beats per chord, moving from one to the next without breaking tempo:

Am, Fm, C#m, F#m, G#m, Dm

SECTION SIX

1 minute 1) WITH THE GUITAR, play the following dominant seventh chords, four beats per chord, moving from one to the next without breaking tempo:

F7, C#7, A7, D7, B7, G7

SECTION SEVEN

10 minutes 1) WITH THE GUITAR, follow the instructions given for Section Seven. Record the chords, play them back, and play the harmonic minor scales for the following keys without breaking tempo:

Bm, Gm, Em, Am, Fm, Dm

SECTION EIGHT

10 minutes 1) WITH THE GUITAR, follow the instructions for the exercise which alternates the chord and scale forms from Chapters Three and Four from line to line (page 82) and record the chords, play back, and play the harmonic minor scales for the following keys *without breaking tempo*:

C#m, F#m, Bm, Em, Am, Dm

20 mintues   2) WITH THE GUITAR, follow the instructions for the tune using combined chord scale forms at the end of this chapter (page 85). Record the progression, play it back, and play the appropriate major and minor scales, where indicated, using any of the patterns you have learned so far but with *NO MISTAKES* and *WITHOUT BREAKING TEMPO* at any time. If you cannot complete this exercise in the time allotted without mistakes, slow down the metronome, record the chords again, and play the scales at the slower tempo until you can complete the exercise.

OVERALL TIME LIMIT
65 MINUTES

Chapter Five

INSTRUCTION FIVE:

Go to the test at the end of Chapter Five (page 98). If you can complete the test perfectly within the time limit (55 minutes), go immediately to Instruction Six (page 100). If you cannot complete the test as prescribed, go to the first page of Chapter Five (page 88) and continue your study of the book there. Knowing locations of notes on the neck and the staff is absolutely essential to any serious study of music and/or the guitar. *Do not* go to Chapter Six until you can comfortably complete the test at the end of Chapter Five within the time limit (55 minutes).

SECTION ONE

KNOW THE LOCATION OF THE NOTES ON THE FINGERBOARD AND ON THE STAFF

You already know the names of the notes on the guitar fingerboard (see Chapters One and Three). Now we will see where these notes are written on the music staff.

Look at the diagram for the fourth (D) string in Fig. 46. As you go up the neck, the notes rise in pitch. This is shown clearly in music notation: as the pitch rises, the notes get higher on the staff. Notice that the note names (A, B, C, D, E, F, G, A, B, C, etc.) are assigned consecutively to each line and space on the staff, i.e. if 'A' is on a space, then 'B' is on the next higher line, 'C' is on the next space, 'D' is on the line above 'C', and so forth.

FIGURE 46

Look at this diagram for two minutes. Immediately turn to Fig. 47 and complete the top diagram.

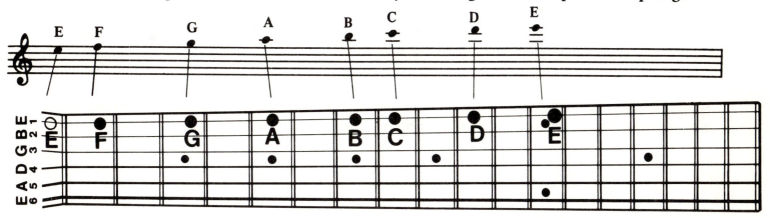

Look at this diagram for two minutes. Turn to Fig. 47 and complete the middle diagram.

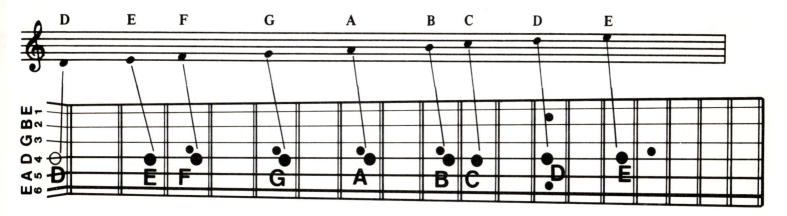

Look at this diagram for two minutes. Turn to Fig. 47 and complete the bottom diagram.

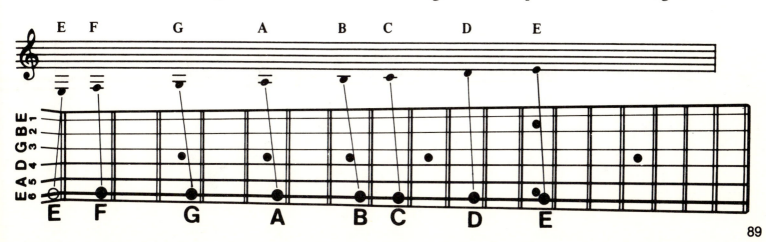

FIGURE 47

Complete this diagram by drawing the notes on the staff that are shown on the fingerboard. Write the note names above the notes. When you have finished, turn to Fig. 48 (next page) and complete the top diagram.

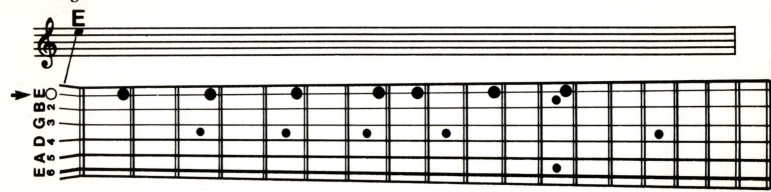

Complete this diagram by drawing the notes on the staff that are shown on the fingerboard. Write the note names above the notes. When you have finished, turn to Fig. 48 and complete the middle diagram.

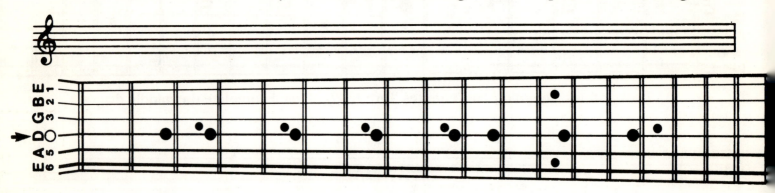

Complete this diagram by drawing the notes on the staff that are shown on the fingerboard. Write the note names above the notes. When you have finished, turn to Fig. 48 and complete the bottom diagram.

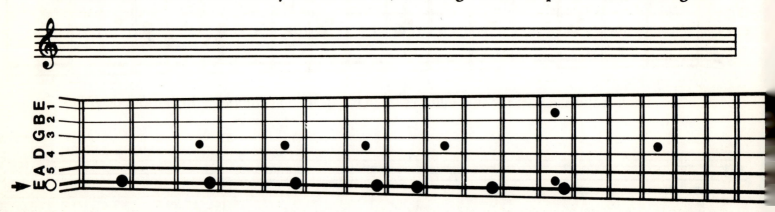

·FIGURE 48

Complete this diagram by drawing dots on the indicated string that correspond to the notes on the staff. Write the note names above the dots on the fingerboard. When you have finished, take a rest break. Then go back to Fig. 46 and follow the instructions above the middle diagram.

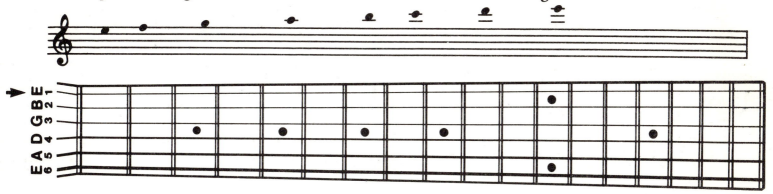

Complete this diagram by drawing dots on the indicated string that correspond to the notes on the staff. Write the note names above the dots on the fingerboard. When you have finished, take a rest break. Then go back to Fig. 46 and follow the instructions above the bottom diagram.

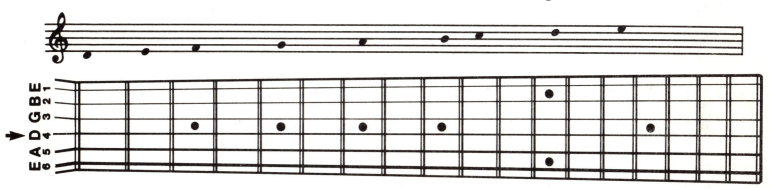

Complete this diagram by drawing dots on the indicated string that correspond to the notes on the staff. Write the note names above the dots on the fingerboard. When you have finished, take a rest break. Then turn to Fig. 49.

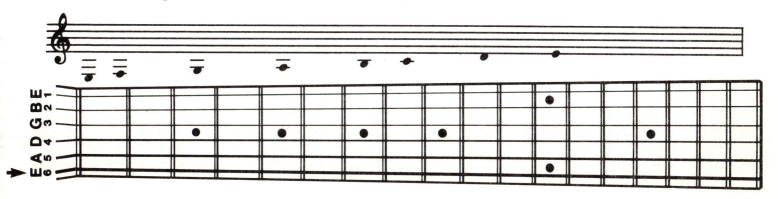

FIGURE 49

Look at this diagram for two minutes. Immediately turn to Fig. 50 and complete the top diagram.

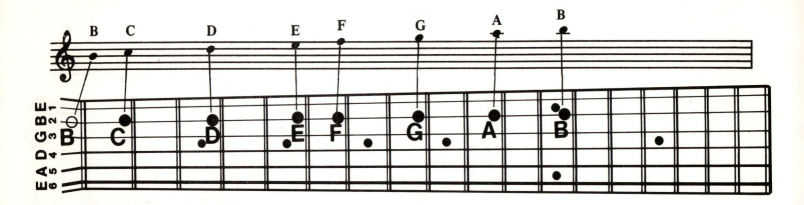

Look at this diagram for two minutes. Immediately turn to Fig. 50 and complete the middle diagram.

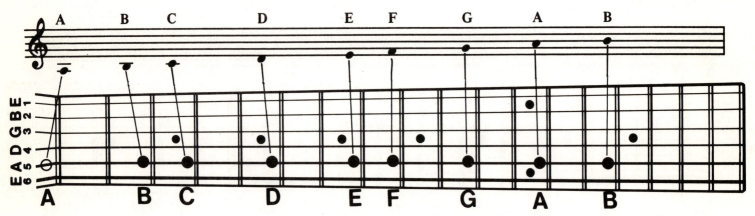

Look at this diagram for two minutes. Immediately turn to Fig. 50 and complete the bottom diagram.

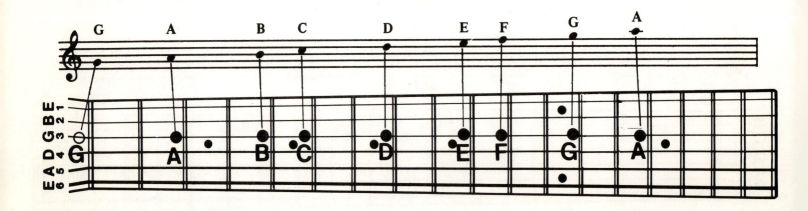

FIGURE 50

Complete this diagram by drawing the notes on the staff that are shown on the fingerboard. Write the note names above the notes. When you have finished, turn to Fig. 51 and complete the top diagram.

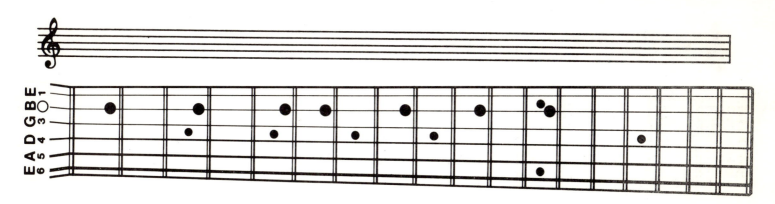

Complete this diagram by drawing the notes on the staff that are shown on the fingerboard. Write the note names above the notes. When you have finished, turn to Fig. 51 and complete the middle diagram.

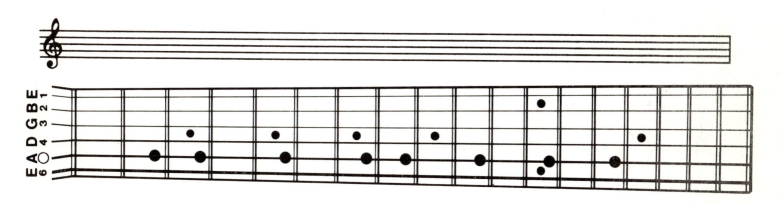

Complete this diagram by drawing the notes on the staff that are shown on the fingerboard. Write the note names above the notes. When you have finished, turn to Fig. 51 and complete the bottom diagram.

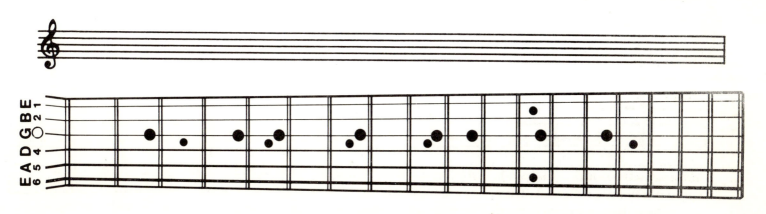

FIGURE 51

Complete this diagram by drawing dots on the indicated string that correspond to the notes on the staff. Write the note names above the dots on the fingerboard. When you have finished, take a rest break. Then go back to Fig. 49 and follow the instructions above the middle diagram.

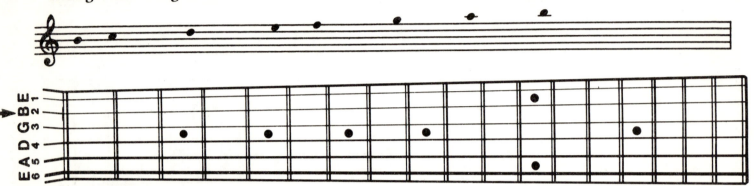

Complete this diagram by drawing dots on the indicated string that correspond to the notes on the staff. Write the note names above the dots on the fingerboard. When you have finished, take a rest break. Then go back to Fig. 49 and follow the instructions above the bottom diagram.

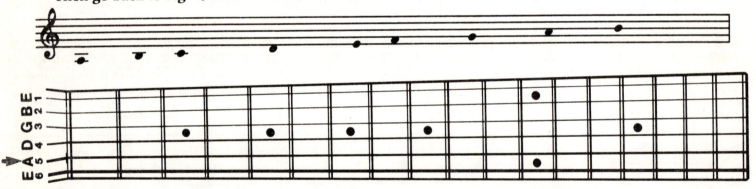

Complete this diagram by drawing dots on the indicated string that correspond to the notes on the staff. Write the note names above the dots on the fingerboard.

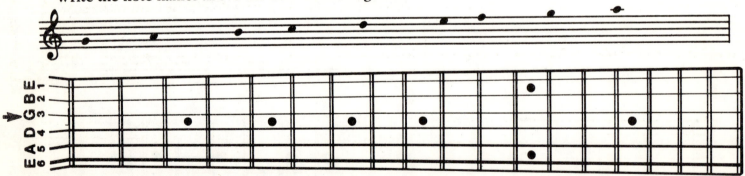

You may have noticed that some notes on any one string are written in the same place on the staff as some notes on a different string. For example, the note on the first fret of the first string is 'F' and is written on the top line of the staff. The note on the sixth fret of the second string is also 'F' and is written on the top line of the staff. This is no reason to panic. If you play both notes, they sound alike: you have found two places on the guitar to play that one pitch.

94

SECTION TWO

KNOW THE LOCATION OF ACCIDENTALS ON THE FINGERBOARD AND ON THE STAFF

In the previous section, you found the natural notes (no sharps or flats) on the guitar and on the staff. Recall the fingerboard diagrams. Wherever there is an empty fret between two notes, it is occupied by an accidental. It has two names - the lower note sharped or the upper note flatted (see the second fret on the first diagram below).

Complete the following diagrams, writing in both names and both staff locations for each accidental (note that the only places where there are no accidentals are all between the notes E and F and the notes B and C).

DRILL: Play the following exercises on the indicated strings. Don't worry about maintaining a steady tempo. Before you leave the note you're playing right now, know *exactly* where you're going to play the next note: no mistakes allowed.

FIRST STRING

SECOND STRING

THIRD STRING

FOURTH STRING

FIFTH STRING

SIXTH STRING

CHAPTER FIVE-END TEST

Review the instructions for the test at the end of Chapter One. As always, DO NOT GO ON TO THE NEXT CHAPTER until you have completed the test within the time allotted. Check the overall time limit at the bottom of the test before you start.

SECTION ONE

4 minutes 1) The following notes are all located on the first string. Write them on the staff in their proper location, then play them in order on the guitar, in tempo, one note for every four beats of the metronome:

D, G, F, B, E, A

4 minutes 2) The following notes are all located on the fourth string. Write them on the staff in their proper location, then play them in order on the guitar, in tempo, one note for every four beats of the metronome.

G, B, D, A, C, E

4 minutes 3) The following notes are all located on the sixth string. Write them on the staff and then play them as above.

C, E, G, B, D, F

4 minutes 4) The following notes are all located on the fifth string. Write them on the staff and then play them as above:

D, G, C, F, A, E

4 minutes 5) The following notes are all located on the second string. Write them on the staff and then play them as above:

E, G, A, C, F, B

4 minutes 6) The following notes are all located on the third string. Write them on the staff and then play them as above:

A, E, B, F, C, G

SECTION TWO

4 minutes 1) The following notes are all located on the first string. Write them on the staff in their proper location, then play them in order on the guitar, in tempo, one note for every four beats of the metronome:

A#, Db, F#, Eb, Bb, G#

4 minutes 2) The following notes are all located on the fourth string. Write them on the staff and then play them as above:

Eb, G#, Ab, C#, F#, Bb

4 minutes 3) The following notes are all located on the sixth string. Write them on the staff and then play them as above:

C#, Eb, Gb, Bb, D#, F#

4 minutes 4) The following notes are all located on the fifth string. Write them on the staff and then play them as above:

Db, G#, F#, Bb, Eb, A#

4 minutes 5) The following notes are all located on the third string. Write them on the staff and then play them as above:

Ab, Eb, Bb, F#, C#, Gb

4 minutes 6) The following notes are all located on the second string. Write them on the staff and then play them as above:

Eb, G#, Ab, C#, F#, Bb

OVERALL TIME LIMIT
55 MINUTES

Chapter Six

INSTRUCTION SIX:

Go to the test at the end of Chapter Six (page 102). If you can complete the test comfortably within the time limit (90 seconds) *without mistakes*, go immediately to Instruction Seven on page 103. If not, go to the first page of Chapter Six (page 101) and continue your study of the book there. Observe the time limit on the test strictly; recall of this information must not only be accurate but quick in order to apply it effectively. DO NOT GO ON TO THE NEXT CHAPTER until you can comfortably complete the test at the end of Chapter Six within the time limit (90 seconds).

SECTION ONE

KNOW HOW MAJOR SCALES ARE BUILT

The major scale (also called the diatonic scale) is the familiar "do-re-mi-fa-so-la-ti-do". It is the first scale you were shown in this book. If this scale were to be played on one string, from any fret (see Fig. 52), it would be built like this:

From the starting note (which is the tonic, or name of the scale), go up two frets (also called two half steps or one whole step) to find the second note. From there, go up two more frets to find the third note. The fourth is one fret (one half step) above the third note. The fifth is two frets (one whole step) above the fourth; the sixth is one whole step above the fifth; the seventh is one whole step above the sixth; and the eighth is one half step above the seventh. The eighth note is the same as the first note, one octave higher in pitch ("octave" is derived from the Latin for "group of eight"). It has the same name, and functions as the starting note of the same scale an octave higher.

FIGURE 52

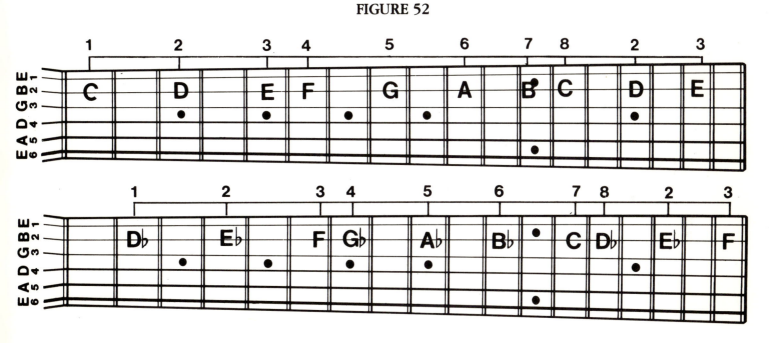

Figure 53 below shows the C major scale in two octaves as it appears on the staff. Note the half steps between 3 and 4, and 7 and 8 as indicated by the arcs.

FIGURE 53

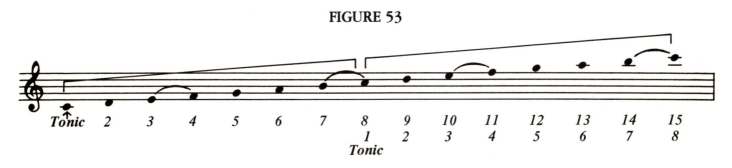

DRILL: Write the letter name of each note above it. Note that 8 and 1 (the tonics) have the same letter name. Likewise, 9 and 2 are the same, as are 10 and 3, 4 and 11, 5 and 12, 6 and 13, and so on. The importance of knowing that 9 and 2, 6 and 13 etc. are the same is that these numbers are used in naming chords.

CHAPTER SIX-END TEST

1) What is the sixth scale step of the C major scale? _____

2) What is the ninth scale step of the C major scale? _____

3) What is the eleventh scale step of the C major scale? _____

4) What is the third scale step of the C major scale? _____

5) What is the seventh scale step of the C major scale? _____

6) What is the fifth scale step of the C major scale? _____

7) What is the thirteenth scale step of the C major scale? _____

8) What is the fourth scale step of the C major scale? _____

OVERALL TIME FRAME
90 SECONDS

NOTE: As always, DO NOT GO ON TO THE NEXT CHAPTER until you can complete this test perfectly in the time allotted.

Chapter Seven

INSTRUCTION SEVEN:

Go to the test at the end of Chapter Seven (page 109). If you can complete the test within the time limit and entirely free of mistakes, go immediately to Instruction Eight on page 111. If not, go to the first page of Chapter Seven (page 104) and continue your study of the book there. Remember: it doesn't matter how long it takes you to master the information in Chapter Seven; but you must eat it and sleep it until it is totally committed to memory. DO NOT GO TO CHAPTER EIGHT until you can complete the test at the end of Chapter Seven within the time limit (30 minutes).

SECTION ONE

WRITE MAJOR SCALES IN MUSIC NOTATION

There are twelve pitches in a given octave. This can be demonstrated by placing your finger anywhere on the fingerboard and moving it twelve consecutive frets in either direction (provided you don't run out of room). The note on the thirteenth fret will have the same name as the starting note. A major scale can be started from any note. In this chapter we will show how to write these scales in music notation.

Suppose we want to write a major scale starting on the note F. First we locate and write F on the staff, then write a note on each consecutive line and space until we get to the next F. (see Fig. 54).

FIGURE 54

Now we number these notes 1 - 8 (see Fig. 55)

FIGURE 55

We recall from the previous chapter that a major scale is made up of all whole steps except for the half steps between 3 and 4 and 7 and 8. Now let's see if our F scale corresponds to this rule by asking the following questions:

Q: Is there a whole step between F/1 and G/2? (refer to the guitar if necessary).   A: Yes. G/2 is OK.

Q: Is there a whole step between G/2 and A/3?   A: Yes. A/3 is OK.

Q: Is there a half step between A/3 and B/4?   A: No. B/4 is a half step too high.
SOLUTION: Lower the B a half step by flatting it. Write the flat in front of the B (see Fig. 56).

FIGURE 56

Q: Is there a half step between A/3 and Bb/4?   A: Yes. Bb/4 is OK.

Q: Is there a whole step between Bb/4 and C/5?   A: Yes. C/5 is OK. (remember that there is a naturally occurring half step between B and C, therefore Bb to C is a whole step.)

Q: Is there a whole step between C/5 and D/6?   A: Yes. D/6 is OK.

Q: Is there a whole step between D/6 and E/7?   A: Yes. E/7 is OK.

Q: Is there a half step between E/7 and F/8?   A: Yes, because remember there is a natural half step between E and F. F/8 is OK.

Now we have completed the scale in one octave. Because there is always a Bb in the key of F, to save the trouble of writing the flat sign every time it occurs we put it at the front of the piece of music next to the treble clef and know that it applies to the whole piece. In other words, it becomes the "key signature" for the key of F. (see Fig. 57)

FIGURE 57

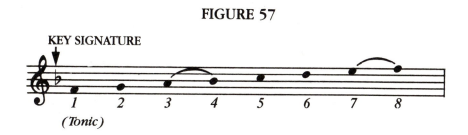

We will now repeat the process for a scale starting on the note D. First locate and write D on the staff, then write a note on each consecutive line and space until you get to the next D (see Fig. 58).

FIGURE 58

Now number the notes 1 - 8 (see Fig. 59).

FIGURE 59

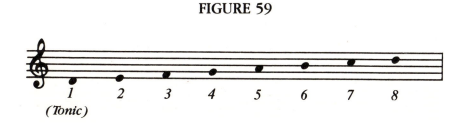

Now see if the D scale corresponds to the necessary whole step/half step layout by asking the same questions we asked about the F scale:

Q: Is there a whole step between D/1 and E/2? A: Yes. E/2 is OK.

Q: Is there a whole step between E/2 and F/3? A: No. F/3 is a half step too low. SOLUTION: raise the F a half step by sharping it. Write the sharp in front of the F. (see Fig. 60).

FIGURE 60

Q: Is there a whole step between E/2 and F#/3? A: Yes. F#/3 is OK.

Q: Is there a half step between F#/3 and G/4? A: Yes. G/4 is OK.

Q: Is there a whole step between G/4 and A/5? A: Yes. A/5 is OK.

Q: Is there a whole step between A/5 and B/6? A: Yes. B/6 is OK.

Q: Is there a whole step between B/6 and C/7? A: No (because of the naturally occurring half step between B and C). C/7 is a half step too low. SOLUTION: raise the C a half step by sharping it. Write the sharp in front of the C (see Fig. 61).

FIGURE 61

Q: Is there a whole step between B/6 and C#/7? A: Yes. C#/7 is OK.

Q: Is there a half step between C#/7 and D/8? A: Yes. D/8 is OK.

Now we have completed the D scale in one octave. As with the flat in the key of F, there will always be an F# and a C# in the key of D major, so we put those two sharps at the front of the music next to the treble clef and know that they apply to the whole piece. Therefore they are the "key signature" for the key of D. (see Fig. 62)

FIGURE 62

Complete the scales below using the process shown for the keys of F and D. When writing multiple sharps or flats in the key signature, they are put in a standard order as shown below:

KEY SIGNATURES

FLAT KEYS				SHARP KEYS		
TONIC OF SCALE	NUMBER OF FLATS	NOTATION		TONIC OF SCALE	NUMBER OF SHARPS	NOTATION
F	1			G	1	
Bb	2			D	2	
Eb	3			A	3	
Ab	4			E	4	
Db	5			B	5	
Gb	6			F#	6	

Because of the natuarally occurring half steps between E and F and B and C, the key of C requires no sharps or flats in the key signature. Verify this using the process already shown.

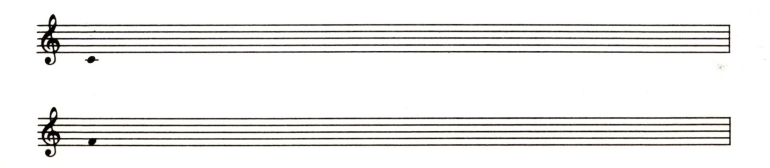

DRILL #1

1) What is the fifth scale step of each of the following keys?

C, Eb, G, D, A, Bb

2) What is the third scale step of each of the following keys?

F, Db, E, Ab, B, Gb

3) What is the sixth scale step of each of the following keys?

D, G, C, F, Ab, Eb

4) What is the fourth scale step of each of the following keys?

E, Bb, A, Gb, Db, B

DRILL #2

1) How many sharps in the key of A?

2) How many flats in the key of Bb?

3) How many sharps in the key of D?

4) How many flats in the key of Ab?

5) How many sharps in the key of G?

6) How many flats in the key of Gb?

7) How many sharps in the key of E?

8) How many flats in the key of F?

9) How many sharps in the key of B?

10) How many flats in the key of Eb?

11) How many sharps in the key of F#?

12) How many flats in the key of Db?

13) How many sharps in the key of C?

DRILL #3

1) The note C is what scale step number of the following keys?

Db, G, Ab, F, Bb, C, Eb

2) The note Bb/A# is what scale step number of the following keys?

F, Ab, Gb, Bb, Eb, Db, B, F#

3) The note G is what scale step number of the following keys?

Eb, Bb, D, G, C, Ab, F

4) The note F is what scale step number of the following keys?

Bb, C, Gb, Ab, Db, Eb, F

5) The note D is what scale step number of the following keys?

C, Eb, G, F, Bb, A, D

6) The note Eb/D# is what scale step number of the following keys?

F#, Bb, Eb, Ab, Db, Gb, B, E

7) The note E is what scale step number of the following keys?

A, F, C, G, D, E, B

8) The note Ab/G# is what scale step number of the following keys?

E, Db, A, Ab, B, F#, Eb, Gb

9) The note B is what scale step number of the following keys?

C, G, D, E, A, F#, B

10) The note A is what scale step number of the following keys?

F, Bb, C, G, E, D, A

11) The note Db/C# is what scale step number of the following keys?

E, D, Ab, Gb, B, Db, A, D

12) The note Gb/F# is what scale step number of the following keys?

B, Db, G, D, A, E, Gb, F#

CHAPTER SEVEN-END TEST

Review the instructions for the test on Chapter One. DO NOT GO ON TO THE NEXT CHAPTER until you can complete this test perfectly in the time allotted. Check the overall time limit at the end of the test *before* you begin: adhere to it strictly.

SECTION ONE

Write out the major scales for the following keys, one octave each. Include on the staff:

1) key signature
2) names of the notes
3) scale step numbers

NOTE: the first note of each scale is given; you complete the rest.

OVERALL TIME LIMIT
30 MINUTES

Chapter Eight

INSTRUCTION EIGHT:

Go to the test at the end of Chapter Eight (page 128). If you can complete the test comfortably within the time limit and free of mistakes, go immediately to Instruction Nine on page 129. If not, go to the first page of Chapter Eight and continue your study of the book there (page 112). DO NOT GO TO CHAPTER NINE UNTIL YOU CAN COMPLETE THE TEST AT THE END OF CHAPTER EIGHT PERFECTLY WITHIN THE TIME LIMIT (50 minutes).

SECTION ONE

PLAY A NEW MAJOR SCALE FINGERING PATTERN

Memorize the major scale fingering pattern for the key of C as shown in Fig. 63 below. This is another way of playing the diatonic major scale on the guitar. Notice that the roots are on the fourth and sixth strings. In order to play this major scale pattern in any other key, simply locate the tonic on the fourth and/or sixth string and play the same pattern. When you are comfortable with this fingering pattern look at Fig. 64 below.

FIGURE 63

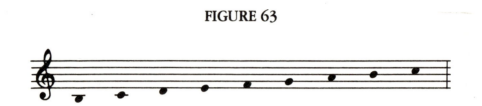

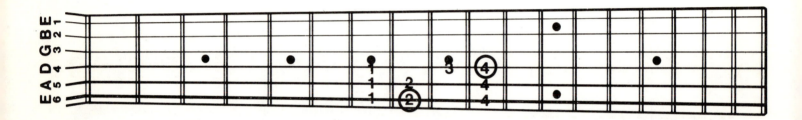

FIGURE 64

Using this new major scale fingering pattern only, play the major scale in each of the keys below (memorize their location on the fingerboard so you can locate them quickly). Using a metronome, play the scales ascending and descending, one note per beat. Make no mistake more than once. (NOTE: you must be able to play all the right notes at exactly the right time - no rushing or dragging. If you set the metronome too fast, i.e. if you find yourself missing notes or playing the notes rhythmically uneven, you will only be slowing your progress by programming mistakes into your playing).

Key of C

Key of E♭

Key of B

Key of D

SECTION TWO

EXPAND THE MAJOR SCALE PATTERN YOU LEARNED IN CHAPTER ONE

Look in Fig. 65 below. A box is drawn around the scale pattern you learned in Chapter One. The remainder of the diagram is the pattern you just learned in the previous section. Notice that the root on the fourth string is part of both patterns. It is the eighth step of the lower octave and the first step of the upper octave (review Chapter Seven if this is unclear).

FIGURE 65

Now look at all the notes in Fig. 65 as one big pattern. This gives you slightly over two octaves in the key of C without shifting positions on the fingerboard. When this is clear in your mind, play slowly through the entire pattern ascending and descending. You should not hesitate at the junction of the two patterns: the notes should flow smoothly throughout the exercise.

Notice the locations of the roots in this big pattern: they are on the first, fourth, and sixth strings. If you want to play in any other key, locate the tonic of the key on any or all of these strings and play this pattern.

When you are comfortable with this way of seeing the full two-octave fingering pattern, look back to Fig. 64. Using this new, expanded fingering pattern only, play the major scale in each of the indicated keys (memorize the locations of the keys on the fingerboard so you can move from one key to the next without disrupting the rhythmic flow). Using a metronome, play the scales ascending and descending, one note per beat. When you play the last note in one key, move immediately (on the next beat of the metronome) to the first note in the next key. Make no mistake more than once.

SECTION THREE

PLAY CHORDS AND MAJOR SCALES TOGETHER IN ALL KEYS

STEP 1: Record the chords below on a tape recorder at a slow to moderate tempo using a metronome. Play each line twice and then go on to the next line without stopping. Hold each chord for four beats on the metronome.

STEP 2: Play back the recorded chord changes and play the indicated scales along with the recording. You may play the notes of the scale in any order.

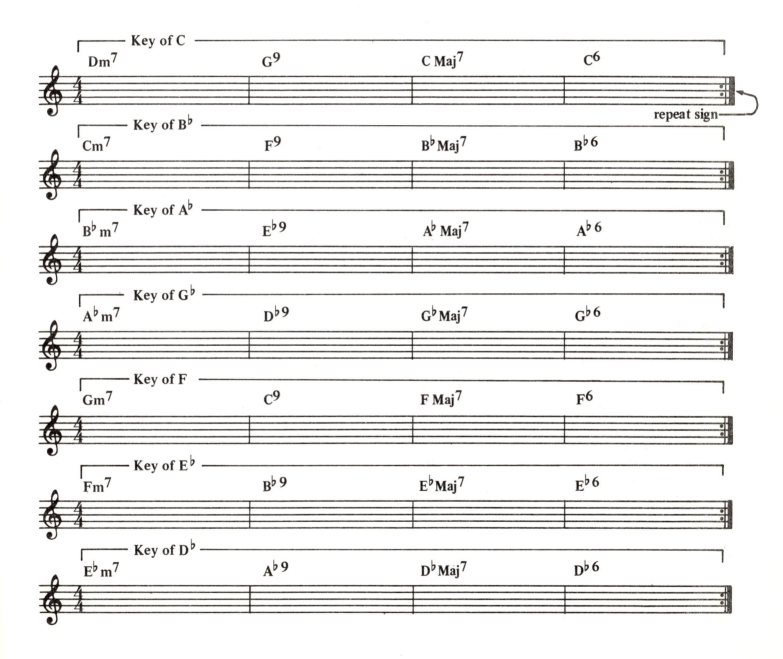

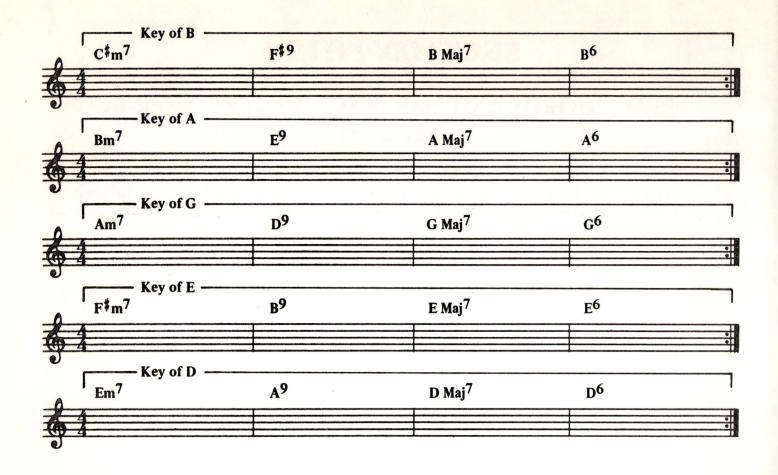

SECTION FOUR

EXPAND THE MAJOR SCALE PATTERN YOU LEARNED IN CHAPTER TWO

Look at Fig. 66 below. The major scale pattern you learned in Chapter Two is enclosed in the box. Now we are adding five notes below the root on the fifth string. Memorize the notes on the fifth and sixth strings in the figure. These are the five new notes plus the root of the pattern from Chapter Two. Play these notes several times ascending and descending. Notice how these notes fit with the pattern you already know.

The lowest note added here is A, which is the third step of this scale (F major). If this is unclear, refer to Chapter Seven.

FIGURE 66

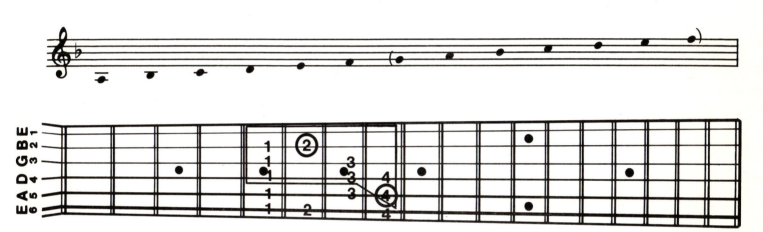

Play the expanded pattern several times very slowly. When you are comfortable with it, look at Fig. 67. Using this expanded major scale pattern only, play the scales in each of the specified keys (memorize their locations on the fingerboard so you can move from one key to the next without hesitation). Using a metronome, play the scales ascending and descending, one note per beat. Remember: make no mistake more than once.

FIGURE 67

(Continued)

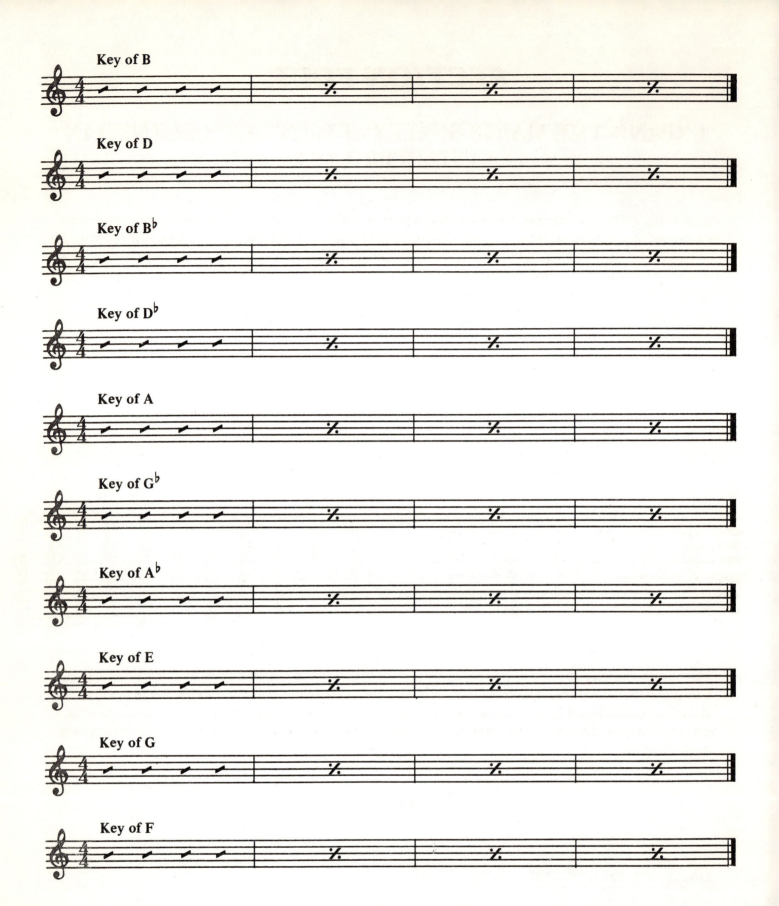

SECTION FIVE

COMPLETE THE EXPANSION OF THE MAJOR SCALE
YOU LEARNED IN CHAPTER TWO

Look at Fig. 68 below. The major scale pattern you learned in Chapter Two is enclosed in the box. Now we are adding four notes above the root on the second string. Memorize the notes on the first and second strings in the figure. These are the four new notes plus the top two notes (the seventh and the root) of the pattern from Chapter Two. Play these notes several times until they feel comfortable. Notice how these notes fit with the pattern you already know.

The highest note added here is C, which is the fifth step of the F major scale.

FIGURE 68

Play the extended pattern as shown in Fig. 68 several times very slowly. When you are comfortable with it, look at Fig. 67. Using this extended pattern only (the pattern from Chapter Two plus the notes we just added on strings 1 and 2), play the scales in each of the indicated keys. Using a metronome, play the scales ascending and descending, one note per beat. Remember: speed is a byproduct of accuracy; set the metronome slow enough that you can play the exercise perfectly.

SECTION SIX

COMBINE THE PATTERNS FROM SECTIONS FOUR AND FIVE

Look at Fig. 69 below. A box is drawn around the patten you learned in Chapter Two. The notes we added in the two previous sections of this chapter are also in the diagram. Notice that the roots are on the second and fifth strings.

Now look at all the notes in the figure as one big pattern. Ths gives you slightly over two octaves in the key of F without shifting positions on the fingerboard. This pattern extends from the third step of the scale upward through two octaves to the fifth step of the scale. When this is clear in your mind, play slowly and smoothly through the entire pattern ascending and descending.

FIGURE 69

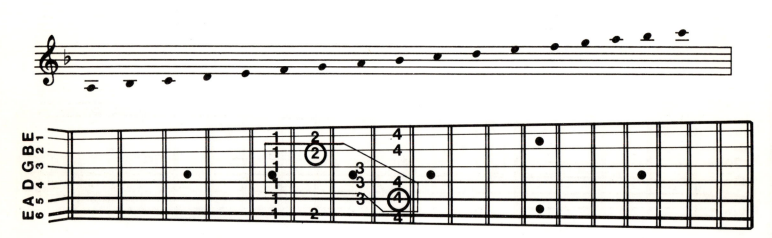

Using this fully expanded fingering pattern only, play the major scale in each of the specified keys shown below. Using a metronome, play one note per beat. When you play the last note in one key, move immediately (on the next beat of the metronome) to the first note in the next key. Remember: attempting to play the exercise faster than you are able to execute it flawlessly will only slow down your progress.

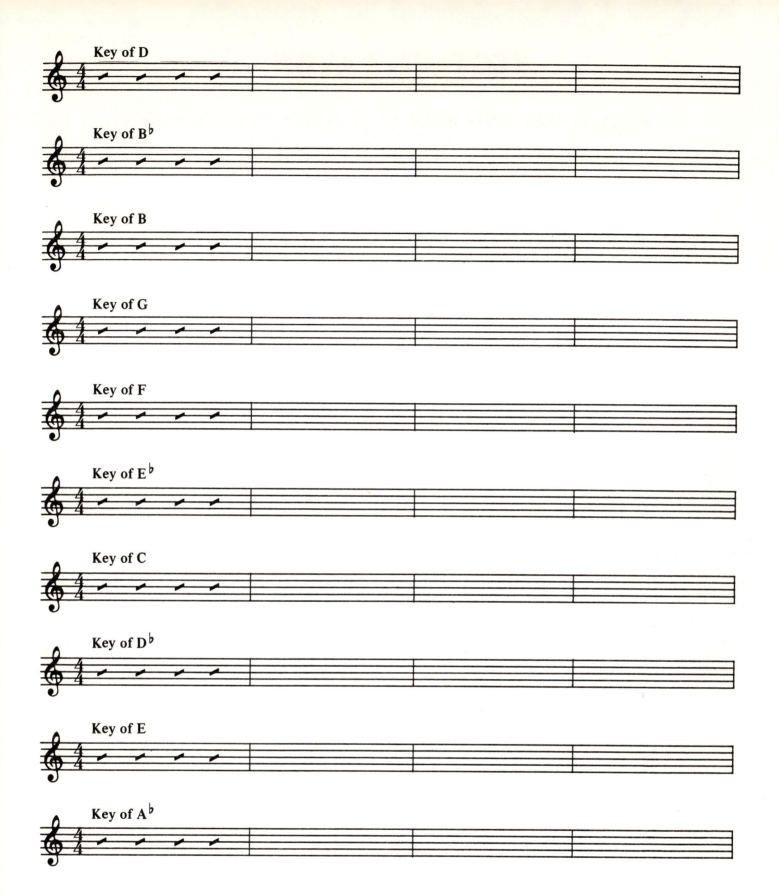

SECTION SEVEN

PLAY CHORDS AND MAJOR SCALES TOGETHER IN ALL KEYS

STEP 1: Record the chords below on a tape recorder at a slow to moderate tempo using a metronome. Play each line twice and then go on to the next line without stopping. Hold each chord for four beats on the metronome.

STEP 2: Play back the recorded chord changes and play the indicated scales along with the recording. You may play the notes of the scale in any order.

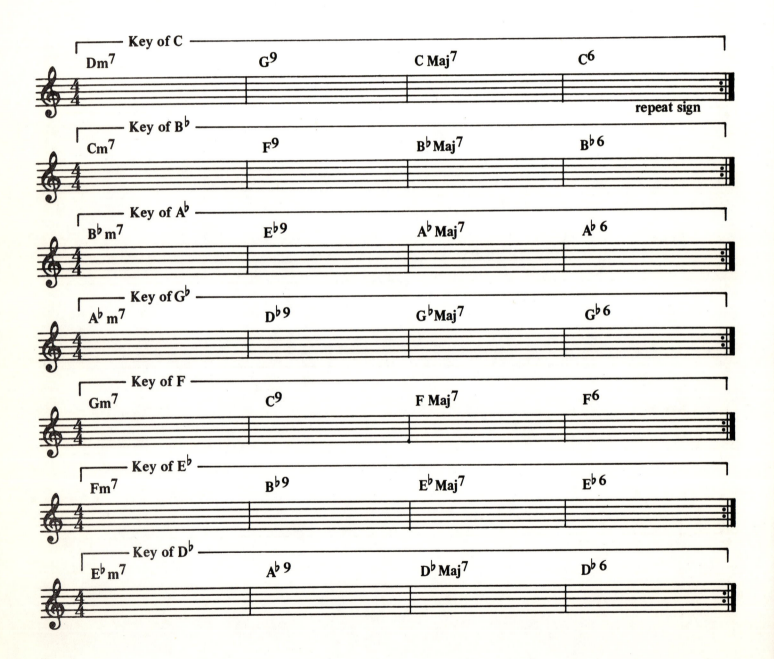

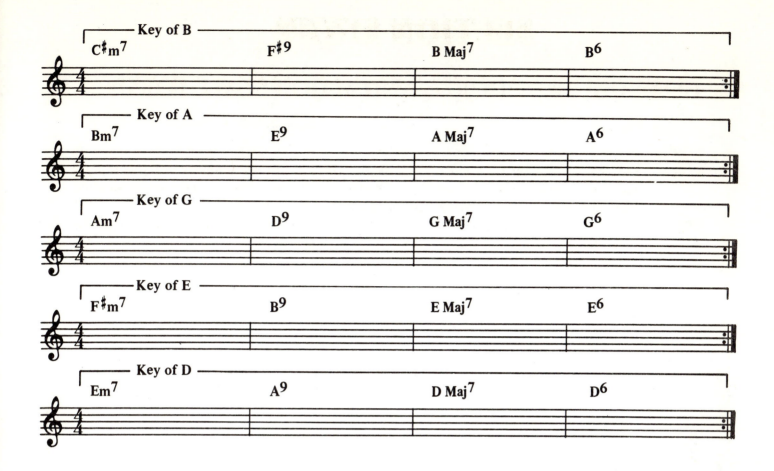

SECTION EIGHT

COMBINE THE CHORDS AND MAJOR SCALE FORMS

STEP 1: Record each line below twice, playing the first time through using the first set of minor, dominant, and major chords learned (Chapter One) and the second time with the second set of chords learned (Chapter Two) DO NOT STOP between chord sets or between keys. Use a metronome setting slow enough to be mistake-proof.

STEP 2: Play back the recorded changes and play the scales for the keys indicated using the pattern learned in Section Two of this chapter (page 114) the first time through and the pattern learned in Section Six of this chapter (page 120) the second time through. Move from one pattern to the next and one key to the next *without breaking tempo*.

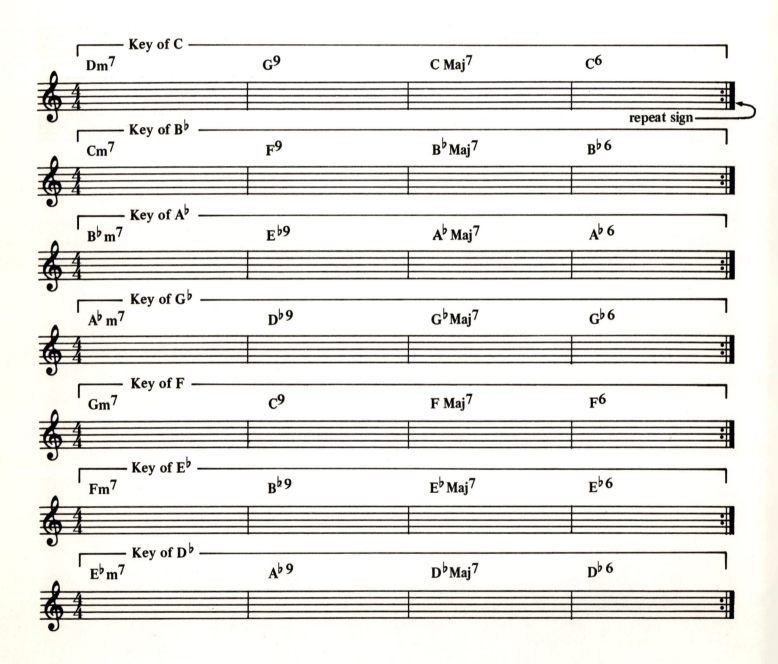

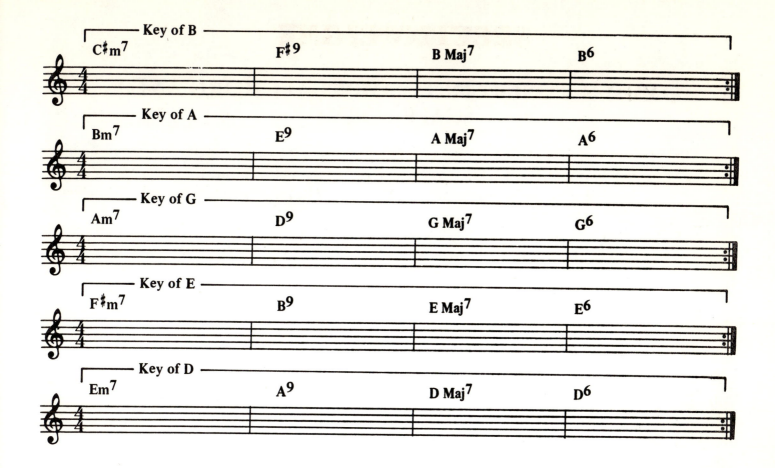

SECTION NINE

PLAY A TUNE USING COMBINED CHORD AND SCALE FORMS

STEP 1: Record the progression below using *any* of the chord forms learned so far, in any combination. Some combinations will obviously be more practical than others, but feel free to experiment.

STEP 2: Play back the recorded changes and play the scales for the keys indicated along with the recording. Use either major scale pattern learned so far. Switch from one to the other where convenient, but do not break tempo. Play the notes in any order. Hold each note for its full value.

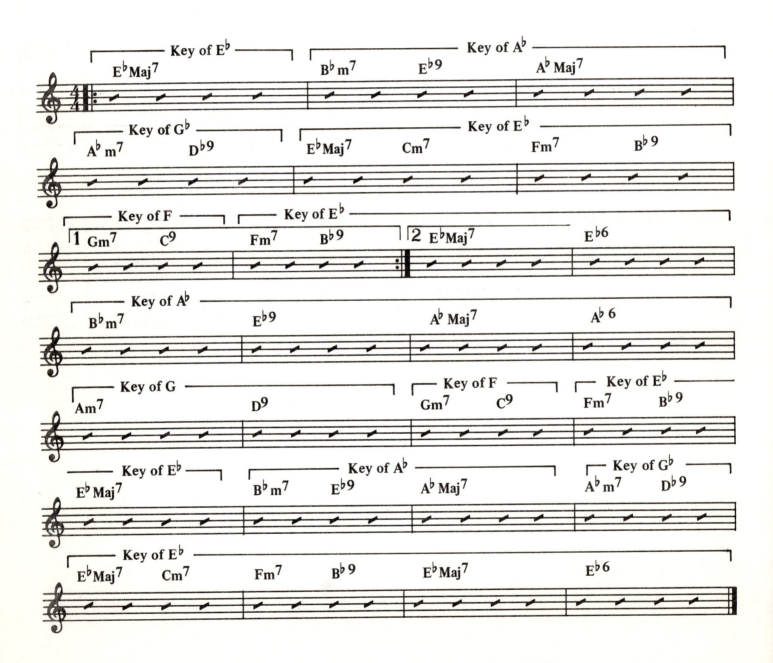

126

Now you know two two-octave fingering patterns for the major scale. If you put both patterns in the same key, you can now cover almost the entire neck in that key. This is shown for the key of G in Fig. 70.

FIGURE 70

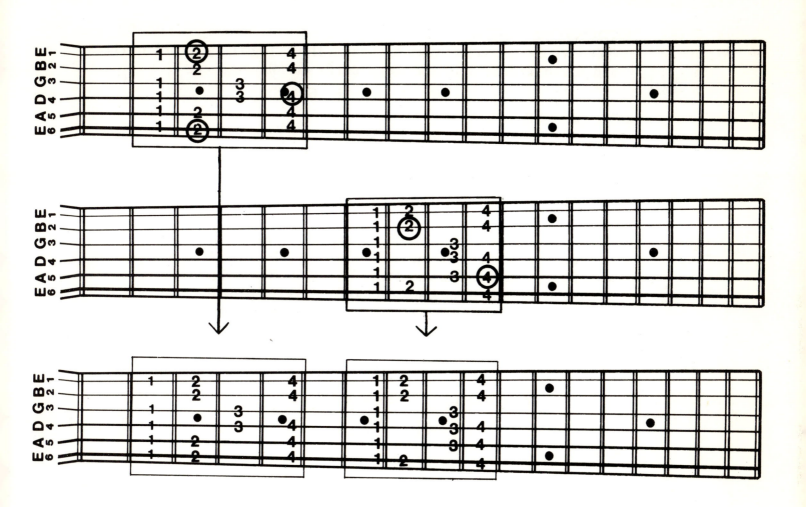

DRILL:

Locate and play both extended patterns in the following keys:

D,   A,   Bb,   Eb

CHAPTER EIGHT-END TEST

Review the instructions for the test at the end of Chapter One. DO NOT GO ON TO THE NEXT CHAPTER until you have completed this test perfectly in the time allotted. Review *only* the sections which are unclear to you; don't waste time going back over things you already know. Note the overall time limit before you begin: adhere to it strictly.

SECTIONS ONE - THREE

10 minutes 1) Following the instructions given for Section Three (page 115), record the chords and play the expanded (two octave) scales for the following keys:

C, D, Bb, E, G, Db

SECTIONS FOUR - SEVEN

10 minutes 1) Following the instructions given for Section Seven (page 122), record the chords and play the major scales in the expanded (two octave) versions for the following keys:

E, G, Bb, Db, A, Eb

SECTIONS EIGHT - NINE

20 minutes 1) Following the instructions given for Section Nine (page 126), record the progression using combined chord and scale forms. Play it back and play the expanded scale forms for the keys indicated with *NO MISTAKES* and *WITHOUT BREAKING TEMPO* at any time. If you cannot complete this exercise in the time allotted without mistakes, slow down the metronome, record the chords again, and play the scales at the slower tempo until you can complete the exercise.

OVERALL TIME LIMIT
50 MINUTES

Chapter Nine

INSTRUCTION NINE:

Go to the test at the end of Chapter Nine (page 176). If you can complete the test comfortably within the time limit (100 minutes) and completely free of mistakes, go immediately to Instruction Ten (page 177). If not, go to the first page of Chapter Nine and continue your study of the book there (page 130). Remember: Speed is the byproduct of Accuracy; play each arpeggio no faster than you can play it perfectly. Do not go to Chapter Ten until you complete the test at the end of Chapter Nine comfortably within the time limit (100 minutes).

SECTION ONE

PLAY THE ARPEGGIOS

An arpeggio is the notes of a chord played one at a time in any order. In the following studies we will start each arpeggio on the root of the chord to develop sure-fire accuracy in positioning the arpeggio shape on the fingerboard. The arpeggio does not *have* to start on the root to maintain its characteristic sound; i.e. a G7 arpeggio sounds like a G7 arpeggio no matter which of its notes you start on.

Look at Fig. 71 below. Memorize the D minor 7 arpeggio (note: these arpeggios correspond to the chords you learned in Chapter One). Locate the roots (circled on the diagram). To play any minor seventh arpeggio, find the root on the sixth string and play this shape.

FIGURE 71

◯ – Root of Arpeggio

DRILL

STEP 1: When you feel comfortable with the minor seventh arpeggio shape, look at the progression below and record the chords as written.

STEP 2: Play back the recorded chords and play the arpeggio of each chord, one note per beat. There should be no wrong notes or hesitations in your arpeggios. If there are, you should re-record the changes at a slower metronome setting.

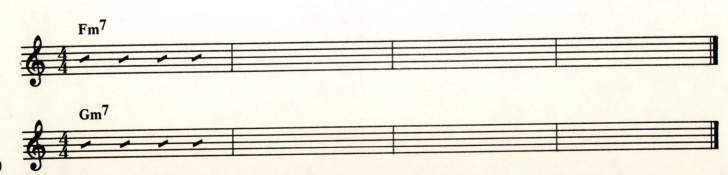

PLAY THE MINOR SEVENTH ARPEGGIO *(Continued)*

THE DOMINANT NINTH ARPEGGIO

Look at the G9 arpeggio in Fig. 72 below and memorize the position of the notes on the fingerboard. Locate the root (circled); to play any dominant ninth arpeggio, find the root on the fifth string and play this shape.

FIGURE 72

DRILL

STEP 1: When you feel comfortable with a dominant ninth arpeggio shape, look at the progression below and record the chords.

STEP 2: Play back the recorded chords and play the arpeggio of each chord, one note per beat. There should be no wrong notes or hesitations in your arpeggios. If there are, you should record the changes again at a slower metronome setting.

THE MAJOR SEVENTH ARPEGGIOS

Memorize the C major seventh arpeggio shown in Fig. 73 below. Locate the roots; to play any major seventh arpeggio, find the root on the sixth string and play this shape.

FIGURE 73

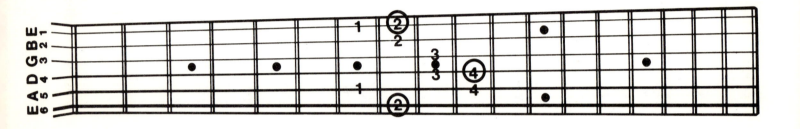

DRILL

    STEP 1: When you feel comfortable with the major seventh arpeggio shape, look at the progression below and record the chords.

    STEP 2: Play back the changes and play the arpeggio of each chord, one note per beat. There should be no wrong beats.

THE MAJOR SIXTH ARPEGGIOS

Memorize the C major sixth arpeggio shown in Fig. 74 below. Locate the roots.

FIGURE 74

DRILL

STEP 1: When you feel comfortable with the major sixth arpeggio shape, record the progession below.

STEP 2: Play back the changes and play the arpeggio of each chord, one note per beat. No wrong notes allowed.

SECTION TWO

PLAY THE ARPEGGIOS AND CHORD IN ALL KEYS

DRILL

STEP 1: Record each line below twice, playing the first time through using the first set of minor, dominant, and major chords learned (Chapter One) and the second time with the second set of chords learned (Chapter Two). *DO NOT STOP* between chord sets or between keys. Use a metronome setting slow enough to be mistake-proof.

STEP 2: Play back the recorded changes and play the arpeggio for each chord indicated, using the arpeggio shapes learned in this section. You may play the notes of the arpeggio in any order. *However*, always dive for the root of the next arpeggio when the chords change.

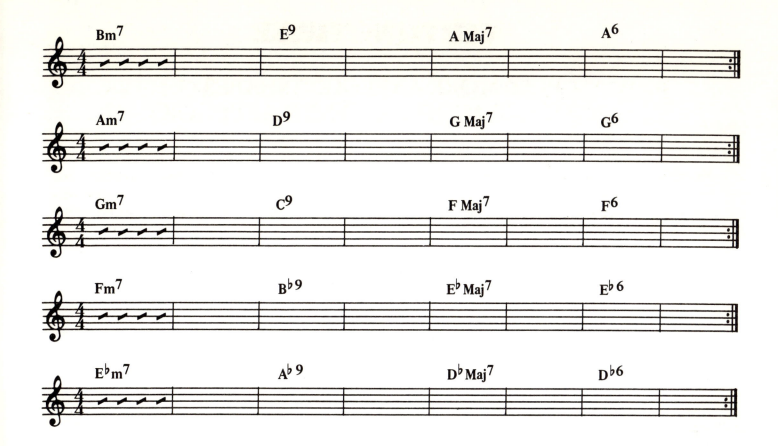

SECTION THREE

PLAY MORE ARPEGGIO SHAPES
ANOTHER MINOR SEVENTH ARPEGGIO

Memorize the G minor seventh arpeggio shown in Fig. 75 below. Note that these arpeggios correspond to the chords you learned in Chapter Two (in the interest of economy of motion, we are starting this particular arpeggio on the fourth rather than the fifth string.) Locate and memorize the position of the root(s).

FIGURE 75

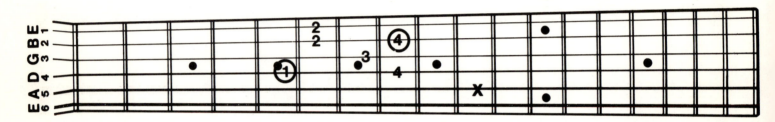

DRILL

STEP 1: When you feel comfortable with this minor seventh arpeggio shape, look at the progression below and record the chords, letting each chord ring for four beats on the metronome.

STEP 2: Play back the recording and play the arpeggio of each chord, one note per beat. No wrong notes, hesitations, string buzzes, etc.

ANOTHER DOMINANT NINTH ARPEGGIO

Memorize the C dominant ninth arpeggio shown in Fig. 76 below. Locate and memorize the position of the root(s).

FIGURE 76

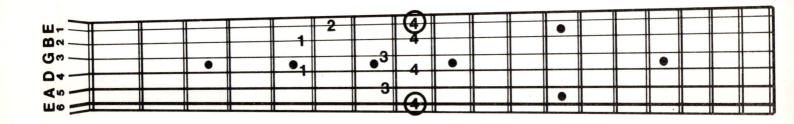

DRILL

STEP 1: When you feel comfortable with this arpeggio shape, record the progression below, letting each chord ring for four beats.

STEP 2: Play back the recording and play the arpeggio of each chord, one note per beat.

ANOTHER MAJOR SEVENTH ARPEGGIO

Memorize the F major seventh arpeggio shown in Fig. 77 below. Locate and memorize the position of the root(s).

FIGURE 77

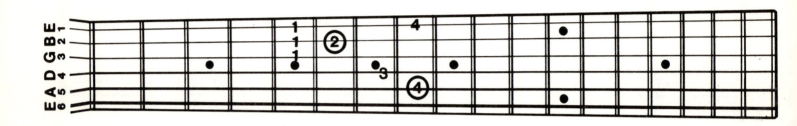

DRILL

STEP 1: When you feel comfortable with this arpeggio shape, record the progression below, letting each chord ring for four beats on the metronome.

STEP 2: Play back the recording and play the arpeggio of each chord, one note per beat, no mistakes, not ahead of or behind the beat.

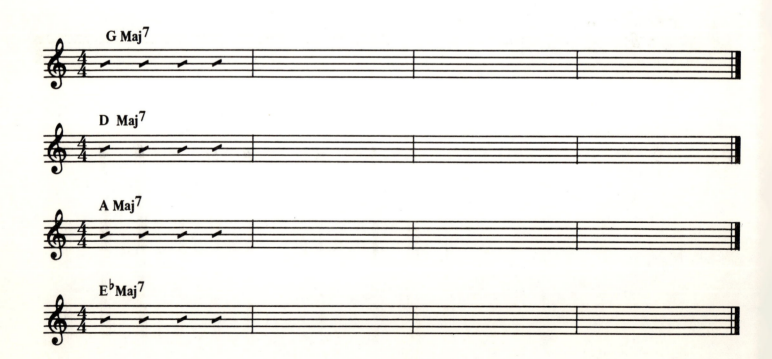

145

ANOTHER MAJOR SIXTH ARPEGGIO

Memorize the F major sixth arpeggio shown in Fig. 78 below. Locate and memorize the position of the root(s).

FIGURE 78

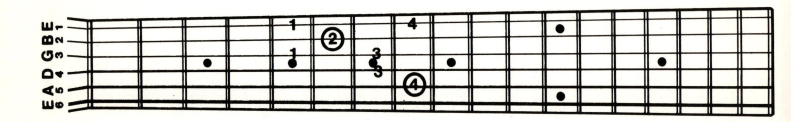

DRILL

STEP 1: When you feel comfortable with this arpeggio shape, record the progression below, letting each chord ring for four beats on the metronome.

STEP 2: Play back the recording and play the arpeggio of each chord, one note per beat, no hesitation.

SECTION FOUR

PLAY THE ARPEGGIOS AND CHORDS IN ALL KEYS

DRILL

> **STEP 1:** Record each line below twice, playing the first time through using the first set of minor, dominant and major chords learned (Chapter One) and the second time through with the second set of chords learned (Chapter Two). DO NOT STOP between chord sets or between keys. Use a metronome setting slow enough to be mistake-proof.
>
> **STEP 2:** Play back the recorded changes and play the arpeggio for each chord indicated, using the arpeggio shapes learned in this section. You may play the notes of the arpeggio in any order, however, always dive for the root of the next arpeggio when the chords change.

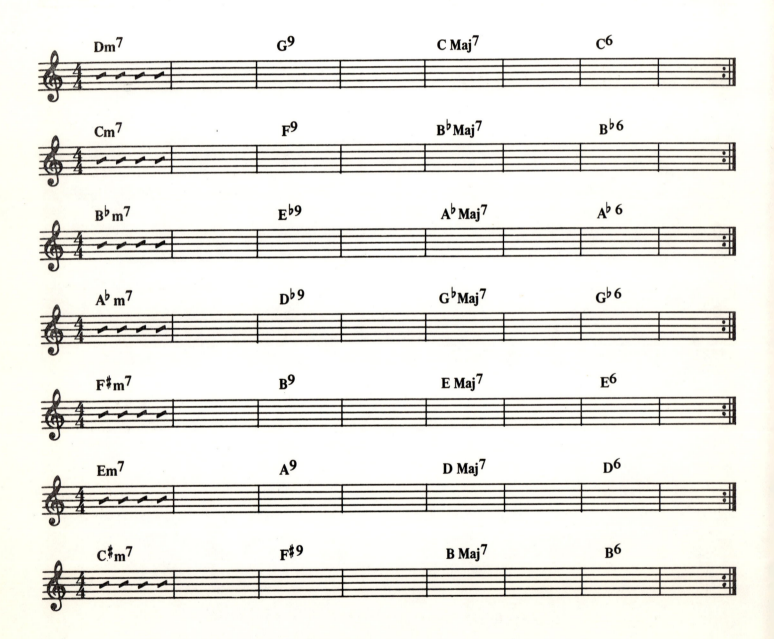

SECTION FIVE

COMBINE THE CHORDS AND ARPEGGIO SHAPES

STEP 1: Record each line below twice playing the first time through using the first set of minor, dominant and major chords learned (Chapter One) and the second time with the second set of chords learned (Chapter Two). DO NOT STOP between chord sets or between keys. Use a metronome setting slow enough to be mistake-proof.

STEP 2: Play back the recorded changes and play the arpeggios of the chords indicated, one note per beat, using the arpeggios learned in Section One of this chapter the first time through and the patterns learned in Section Three of this chapter the second time through. Move from one pattern to the next and one key to the next *without breaking tempo.*

SECTION SIX

PLAY A TUNE USING COMBINED CHORD AND ARPEGGIO FORMS

STEP 1: Record the progression below using any of the chord forms learned so far in any combination.

STEP 2: Play back the recorded changes and play the arpeggios for the chords along with the tape. Use either arpeggio shape learned so far (choose the shapes with an eye toward minimizing position shifts on the fingerboard). You may switch from one set of shapes to the other where convenient, but do not break tempo. Always hit the root of the next arpeggio on the first beat of the next chord.

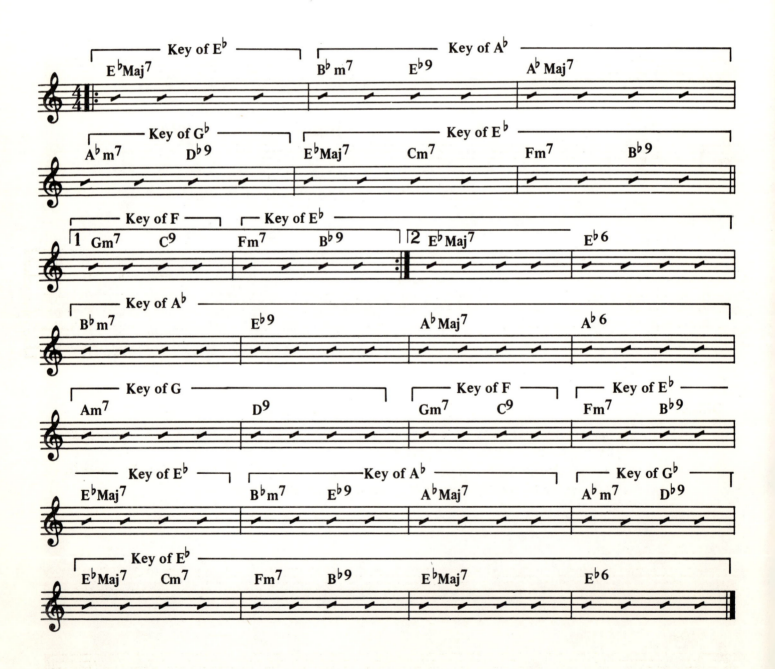

SECTION SEVEN

PLAY EXPANDED ARPEGGIO SHAPES

In the following sections, we will expand the arpeggio shapes you just learned to include all of the notes available in the major scale patterns from Chapter Eight. Up to now, we have started all of the arpeggios on the root of the chord (realizing that they do not *have* to start on the root to sound okay), but with these expanded patterns, the lowest note may not necessarily be the root. In most cases we are adding very few new notes, so it will be easy for you to memorize the expanded shapes. As a result, you will have command of all of the chord tones available within the major scale fingering patterns we have learned, both above and below the roots.

THE EXPANDED MINOR SEVENTH ARPEGGIO

Memorize the D minor seventh arpeggio shown in Fig. 79 below. Locate and memorize the position of the roots (which are the same as previously shown), and locate and memorize the position of any added notes (which were not in the previous shape).

FIGURE 79

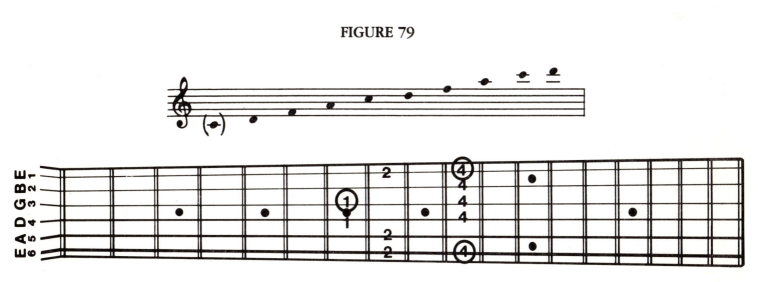

DRILL

STEP 1: When you feel comfortable with the expanded minor seventh shape, record the progression below, letting each chord ring for four beats.

STEP 2: Play back the changes and play the expanded arpeggio of each chord. Play the notes in any order, including the new notes, but allow no mistakes.

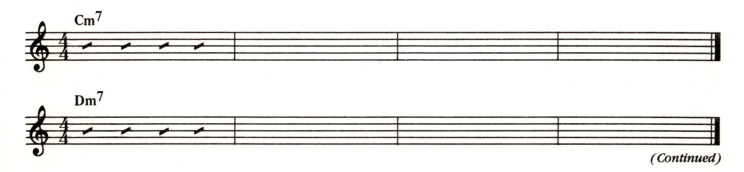

(Continued)

THE EXPANDED DOMINANT NINTH ARPEGGIO

Memorize the expanded G dominant ninth arpeggio shown in Fig. 80 below. Locate the roots and locate and memorize the position of any added notes (not in the previous shape).

FIGURE 80

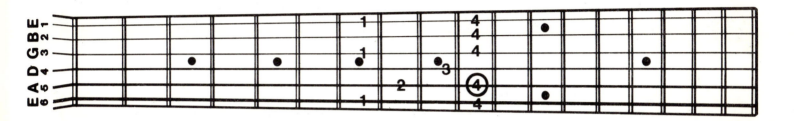

DRILL

    STEP 1:   When you feel comfortable with the expanded dominant ninth arpeggio shape, record the progression below.

    STEP 2:   Play back the changes and play the expanded arpeggio of each chord. Include the added notes but do not include mistakes.

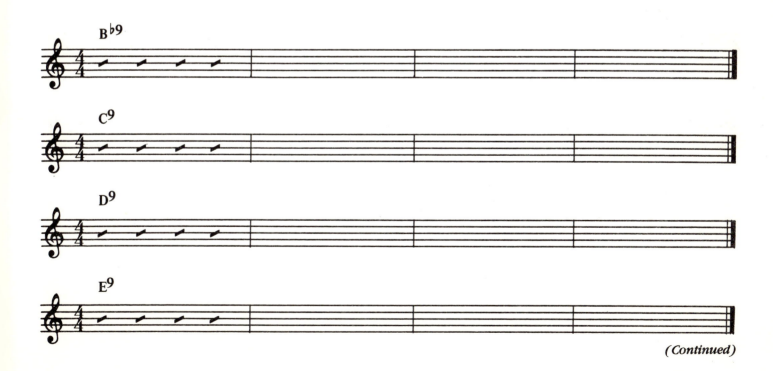

(Continued)

THE EXPANDED MAJOR SEVENTH ARPEGGIO

Memorize the expanded C major seventh arpeggio shown in Fig. 81 below. Locate the roots and locate and memorize the position of any added note(s).

FIGURE 81

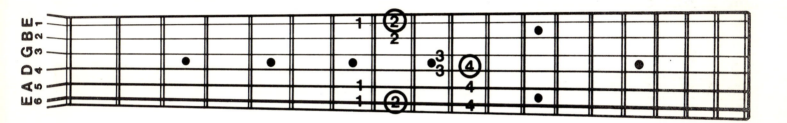

DRILL

STEP 1: Record the progression below, four beats per chord.
STEP 2: Play back the recording and play the expanded arpeggio of each chord. No hesitation, string buzzes, unintended notes.

(Continued)

THE (EXPANDED) MAJOR SIXTH ARPEGGIO

Memorize the C major sixth arpeggio shown in Fig. 82 below. Note that it has no new notes in the "extended" version because all the available chord tones were included in the original version. Use the following drill as a review.

FIGURE 82

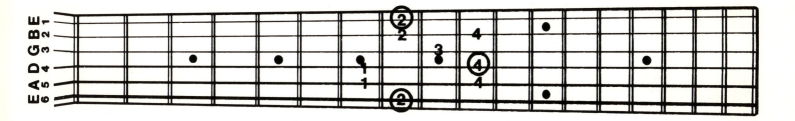

DRILL

STEP 1: Record the progression below.

STEP 2: Play back the recording and play the arpeggio of each chord, one note per beat. Change from chord to chord without hesitation.

(Continued)

SECTION EIGHT

PLAY THE EXPANDED ARPEGGIOS AND CHORDS IN ALL KEYS

DRILL

STEP 1: Record each line below twice, playing the first time through using the first set of minor, dominant and major chords learned (Chapter One) and the second time through with the second set of chords learned (Chapter Two). DO NOT STOP between chord sets or between keys. Mistake-proof your playing.

STEP 2: Play back the recorded changes and play the expanded arpeggio for each chord indicated, using the arpeggio shapes learned in the previous section. Play the notes in any order, including the added notes. Do not hesitate between chords or between keys - keep up a smooth, uninterrupted flow of notes, one per beat.

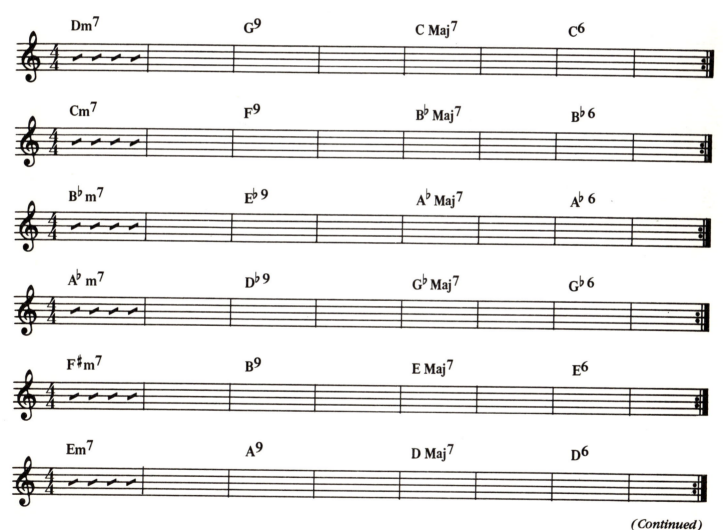

(Continued)

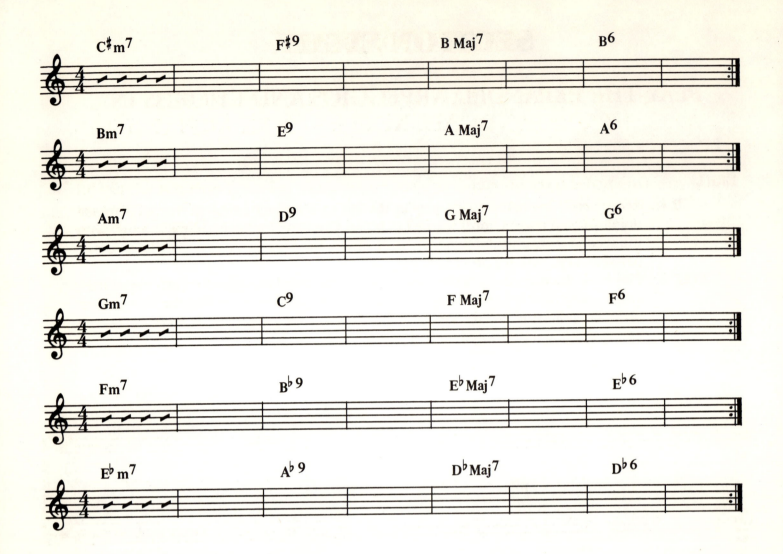

SECTION NINE

PLAY MORE EXPANDED ARPEGGIO SHAPES
ANOTHER EXPANDED MINOR SEVENTH ARPEGGIO

Memorize the expanded G minor seventh arpeggio shown below in Fig. 83. Note that this and the following arpeggios correspond to the chords you learned in Chapter Two. As before, we are adding notes to fill out the shapes to include every available chord tone within the scale pattern. Locate and memorize the root(s) and the position of any new note(s).

FIGURE 83

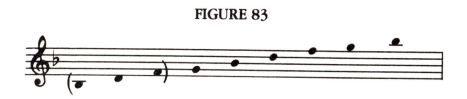

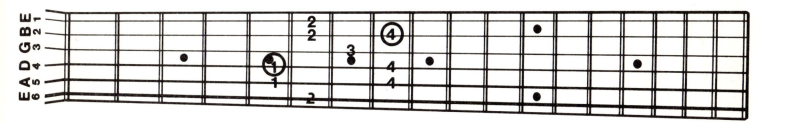

DRILL

    STEP 1:   Record the progression below.

    STEP 2:   Play back the recording and play the arpeggio of each chord, including the added notes. If you make mistakes, go back and record the changes at a slower tempo.

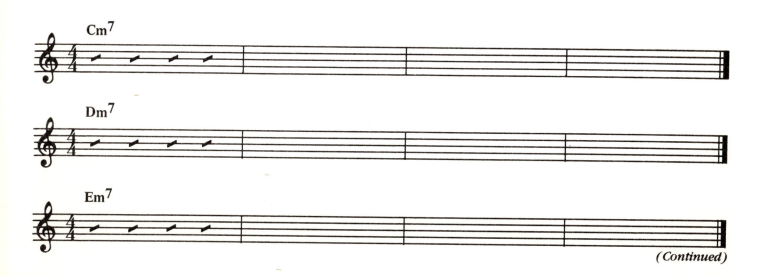

(Continued)

ANOTHER EXPANDED DOMINANT NINTH ARPEGGIO

Memorize the expanded C dominant ninth arpeggio shown in Fig. 84 below. Locate the roots and memorize the position of any added note(s).

FIGURE 84

DRILL

    STEP 1:   Record the progression below.

    STEP 2:   Play back the recording and play the arpeggio of each chord, including the added notes.

(Continued)

ANOTHER EXPANDED MAJOR SEVENTH ARPEGGIO

Memorize the expanded F major seventh arpeggio shown in Fig. 85 below. Locate the roots and memorize the position of any added note(s).

FIGURE 85

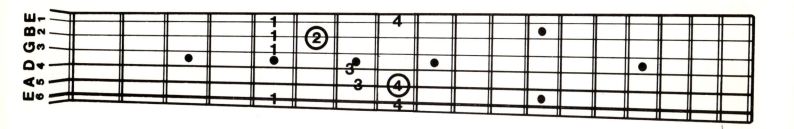

DRILL

STEP 1: Record the progression below.

STEP 2: Play back the recording and play the expanded arpeggio of each chord. No mistakes allowed.

(Continued)

ANOTHER EXPANDED MAJOR SIXTH ARPEGGIO

Memorize the expanded F major sixth arpeggio shown in Fig. 86 below. Locate the roots and memorize the position of any added note(s).

FIGURE 86

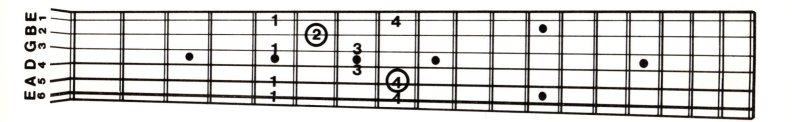

DRILL

STEP 1: Record the progression below, holding each chord for four beats.
STEP 2: Play back the recording and play the expanded arpeggio of each chord. No hesitation between keys.

(Continued)

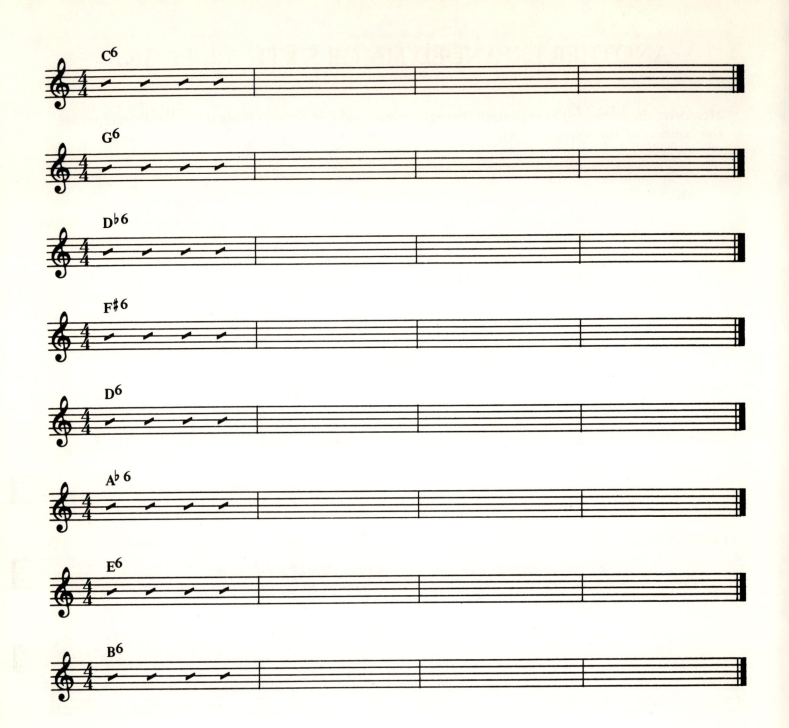

SECTION TEN

PLAY THE EXPANDED ARPEGGIOS AND CHORDS IN ALL KEYS

DRILL

STEP 1: Record each line below twice, playing the first time through using the first set of minor, dominant, and major chords learned (Chapter One) and the second time through with the second set of chords learned (Chapter Two). DO NOT STOP between chord sets or between keys. Use a mistake-proof metronome setting.

STEP 2: Play back the recorded changes and play the expanded arpeggio for each chord using the arpeggio shapes learned in Section Nine. You may play the notes of the arpeggio in any order, however, make sure you make the chord changes accurately, diving for the root of the next arpeggio on the first beat of the next chord if necessary.

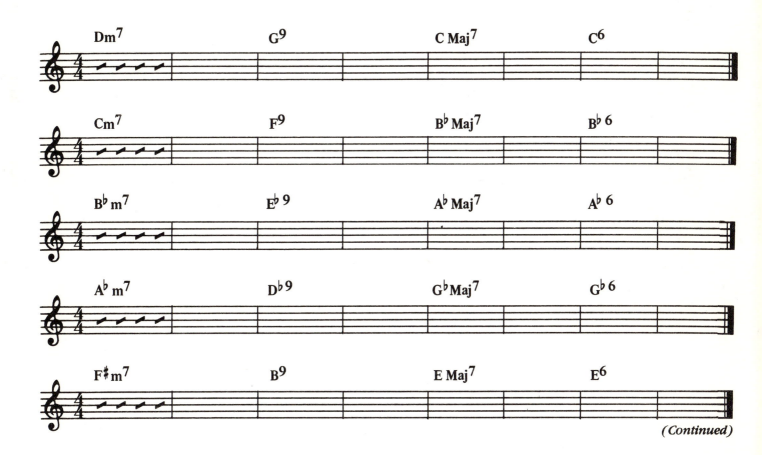

(Continued)

SECTION ELEVEN

COMBINE THE CHORDS AND EXPANDED ARPEGGIO SHAPES

DRILL

STEP 1: Record each line below twice, playing the first set of chords learned (Chapter One) the first time through and the second set of chords learned (Chapter Two) the second time through. DO NOT STOP between chord sets or keys.

STEP 2: Play back the changes and play the expanded arpeggio of each chord, one note per beat, using the arpeggios learned in Section Seven of this chapter the first time through and the arpeggios learned in Section Nine of this chapter the second time through. Move from one pattern to the next and one key to the next *without breaking tempo*.

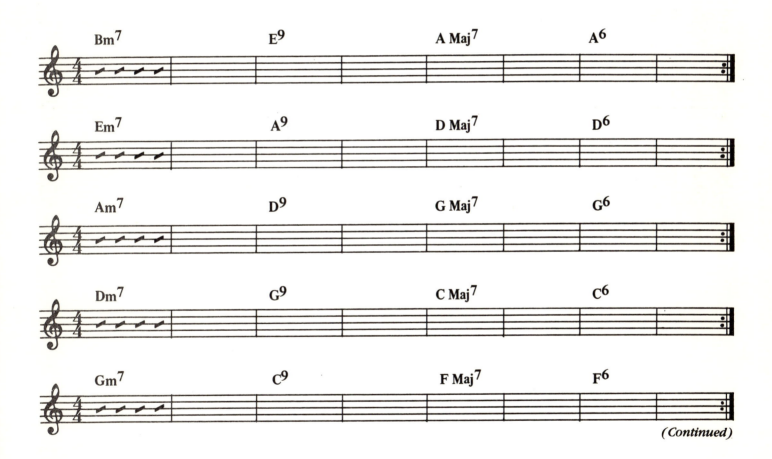

(Continued)

SECTION TWELVE

PLAY A TUNE USING COMBINED CHORD AND EXPANDED ARPEGGIO FORMS

DRILL

STEP 1: Record the progression below using any of the chord forms learned so far in any combination.

STEP 2: Play back the recorded changes and play the arpeggios for the chords along with the tape (including added notes). Use either expanded arpeggio shape learned so far, choosing the shapes with an eye toward minimizing position shifts on the fingerboard. You may switch from one set of shapes to the other where convenient, but do not break tempo. Always hit the root of the next arpeggio on the first beat of the next chord, after which you may play the notes of the arpeggio in any order.

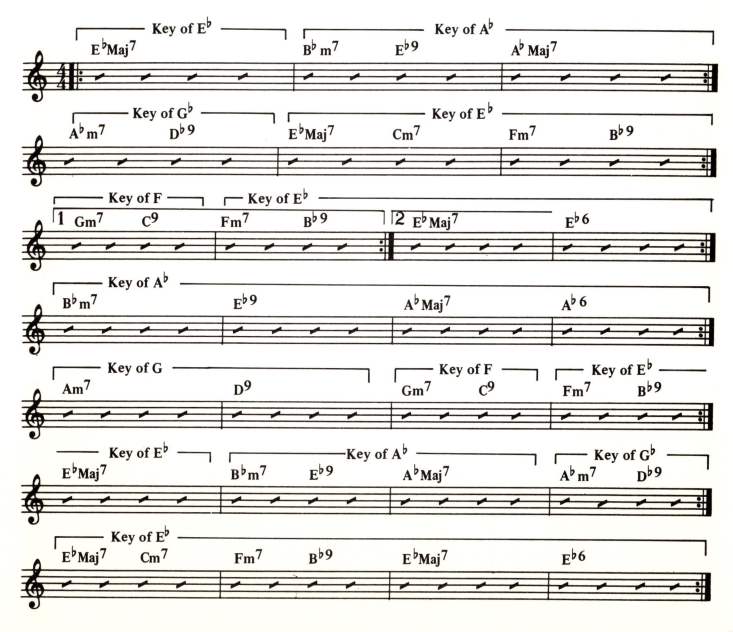

CHAPTER NINE-END TEST

Refer to the instructions for the test at the end of Chapter One. DO NOT GO ON TO THE NEXT CHAPTER until you have completed this test perfectly in the time allotted. Note the overall time limit at the end of this test and adhere to it strictly.

SECTIONS ONE - TWO

10 minutes   1) Following the instructions given for Section Two (page 138), record the chords and play the arpeggios for the following keys. No mistakes or breaks in tempo allowed; if they occur, re-record the changes at a slower tempo and perform the exercise again:

Bb,   Gb,   D,   F

SECTIONS THREE - FOUR

10 minutes   1) Following the instructions given for Section Four (page 148), record the chords and play the arpeggios for the following keys as above:

Ab,   E,   B,   F#

SECTIONS FIVE - SIX

20 minutes   1) Following the instructions for Section Six (page 152), record the progression and play the arpeggios, using either set of arpeggio shapes in any combination. *However:* no mistakes or breaks in tempo are allowed on this test, so use a mistake-proof metronome setting and plan your moves carefully.

SECTIONS SEVEN - EIGHT

10 minutes   1) Following the instructions for Section Eight (page 161), record the chords and play the expanded arpeggios for the following keys as above:

C,   A,   Db,   Eb

SECTIONS NINE - TEN

10 minutes   1) Following the instructions for Section Ten (page 171), record the chords and play the expanded arpeggios for the following keys as above:

B,   Ab,   F,   Eb

SECTIONS ELEVEN - TWELVE

20 minutes   1) Following the instructions for Section Twelve (page 175), record the progression and play the arpeggios, using either set of expanded arpeggios in any combination. Remember: to pass this test, your playing on this exercise must be mistake-free.

Chapter Ten

INSTRUCTION TEN:

Go to the test at the end of Chapter Ten (page 180). If you can complete the test comfortably within the time limit (15 minutes), free of mistakes, go immediately to Instruction Eleven on page 181. If not, go to the first page of Chapter Ten and continue your study of the book there (page 178). Set the metronome at a mistake-proof tempo; *never* faster than you can play perfectly. Do not go to the next chapter until you complete the test at the end of Chapter Ten perfectly and within the time limit (15 minutes).

SECTION ONE

KNOW THE NAMES OF THE NOTES AND SCALE STEP NUMBERS ON THE FINGERBOARD

Why must you know the names of the notes and scale step numbers in all keys? The reason: these letters and scale step numbers are *the* standard language of music in general. The value of being able to locate any note by letter and/or number instantly on the fingerboard is that it enables you to apply any piece of theoretical information such as harmony and theory, chord construction, playing over changes, etc. immediately to the guitar. *Any* study of music is a piece of cake given this ability. (Handy hint: knowing just the locations of scale steps 1, 3, and 5 in each of the two fingering patterns you have learned makes the location of any other scale step number a simple matter; e.g. 4 is one fret above 3, 6 is a whole step above 5, 7 is a half step (one fret) below 1, etc. See Fig. 87 below.).

FIGURE 87

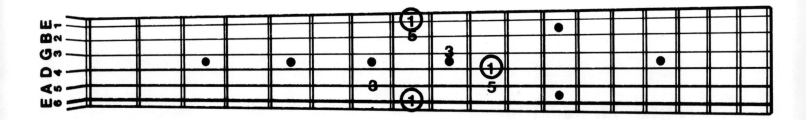

DRILL

Play the following tones in the indicated keys using only the scale pattern you learned in Chapter Eight, Section Two (page 114) (remember: scale step #1 is the tonic):

1) Key of Bb - play all 1's, 3's, and 5's
2) Key of G - play all 1's, 3's, 5's and 4's
3) Key of Eb - play all 1's, 4's, 5's, and 3's
4) Key of C - play all 1's, 3's, 5's, and 2's
5) Key of F - play all 1's, 6's, 5's, and 3's
6) Key of Db - play all 1's, 7's, 3's, and 4's
7) Key of D - play all 1's, 4's, 5's, and 6's
8) Key of E - play all 1's, 2's, 5's, and 3's
9) Key of A - play all 1's, 3's, 5's, and 7's
10) Key of Gb - play all 1's, 3's, 4's, and 5's
11) Key of Ab - play all 1's, 5's, 6's, and 3's
12) Key of B - play all 1's, 3's, 5's and 2's

Look at Fig. 88 below. Memorize the locations of all 1's, 3's, and 5's.

FIGURE 88

DRILL

Play the following tones in the indicated keys using only the scale pattern you learned in Chapter Eight, Section Five (page 119).

1) Key of C - play all 1's, 3's, 5's and 6's
2) Key of F - play all 1's, 3's, 4's, and 5's
3) Key of G - play all 1's, 5's, 2's, and 3's
4) Key of Bb - play all 1's, 7's, 3's, and 5's
5) Key of Eb - play all 1's, 4's, 5's, and 3's
6) Key of Ab - play all 1's, 3's, 5's, and 7's
7) Key of D - play all 1's, 4's, 5's, and 3's
8) Key of A - play all 1's, 3's, 5's, and 4's
9) Key of E - play all 1's, 3's, 2's, and 5's
10) Key of Db - play all 1's, 5's, 6's, and 3's
11) Key of Gb - play all 1's, 3's, 4's, and 5's
12) Key of B - play all 1's, 3's, 7's and 5's

CHAPTER TEN-END TEST

Review the instructions for the test at the end of Chapter One. DO NOT GO ON TO THE NEXT CHAPTER until you have completed this test perfectly in the time allotted. Check the overall time limit at the end of this test before you begin and adhere to it.

6 minutes   1) Referring to the drill beneath Fig. 87, play *all* 1's, 3's, 5's, 7's, 2's, 4's and 6's (in that order) for each of the keys below. Hold each note for two beats of the metronome: *do not* break tempo (you may pause between keys):

Bb, F, C, G, D, A

6 minutes   2) Referring to the drill beneath Fig. 88, play all 1's, 3's, 5's, 7's, 2's, 4's, and 6's (in that order) for each of the keys below. Hold each note for two beats of the metronome; do not break tempo (you may pause between keys):

E, B, Gb, Db, Ab, Eb

OVERALL TIME LIMIT
15 MINUTES

Chapter Eleven

INSTRUCTION ELEVEN:

Go to the test at the end of Chapter Eleven (page 192). If you can complete the test comfortably within the time limit (30 minutes) and entirely mistake-free, go immediately to Instruction Twelve. If not, go to the first page of Chapter Eleven (page 182) and continue your study of the book there. Knowing how to spell chords is absolutely essential to any serious study of music and/or the guitar; you *must* complete the test at the end of Chapter Eleven with absolute accuracy within the time limit (30 minutes) *before* going to Chapter Twelve.

SECTION ONE

KNOW HOW TO CONSTRUCT MAJOR SEVENTH CHORDS

A chord is *any* three (or more) notes played at the same time. However, roughly 95% of the chords used in popular music are built in the following manner:

Every chord has a root. The root is the note on which the chord is based, just as a scale is based on a tonic. Thus the alphabet name of a chord is the same as the alphabet name of its root, for example: A major, C minor, C major, E minor, etc.

To build a major seventh chord, treat the root of the chord as a scale tonic and number the scale steps exactly the way you did in Chapter Seven (see Fig. 89 below):

FIGURE 89

Now take the notes that correspond to the scale step numbers 1, 3, 5, and 7 and write them on the staff in a vertical stack (see Fig. 90):

FIGURE 90

Congratulations! You have just built a G major seventh chord.

Let's build one more major seventh before moving on. To construct an Eb major seventh (also written as Eb maj 7, Eb M7, and Eb MA7), picture an Eb major scale. Simply take the notes that are the 1st, 3rd, 5th, and 7th steps of the scale, stack the notes on top of each other, and you have an Eb Maj 7 chord (see Fig. 91).

DRILL

Following the procedure described above, build the following chords:

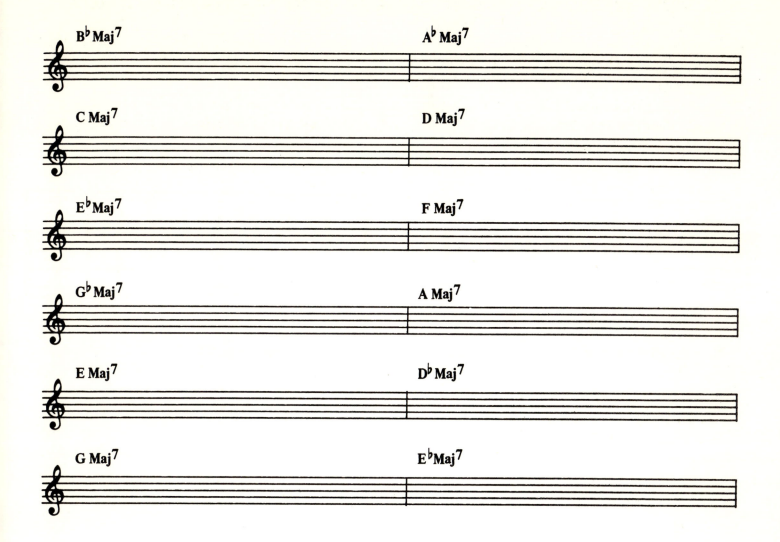

B♭ Maj⁷   A♭ Maj⁷

C Maj⁷   D Maj⁷

E♭ Maj⁷   F Maj⁷

G♭ Maj⁷   A Maj⁷

E Maj⁷   D♭ Maj⁷

G Maj⁷   E♭ Maj⁷

The C maj 7 chord you built in the drill above looks like Fig. 92 below when seen on the staff and the fingerboard:

FIGURE 92

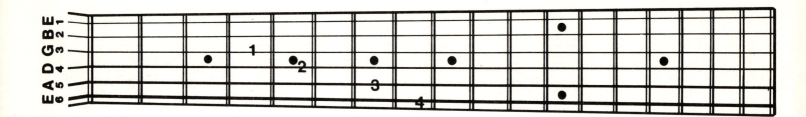

Now recall the C maj 7 chord you learned in Chapter One, Section Five (Fig. 93):

FIGURE 93

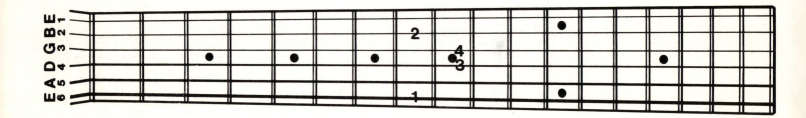

Are both chords built correctly? The answer is yes: both chords include the 1, 3, 5, and 7 of the C major scale (the notes C, E, G, and B), so both fit our formula for a major seventh chord. However, the two chords are different *voicings* of the same chord. To alter the specific sound of a chord, you may voice it with the notes packed closely together (as in Fig. 92) or you may voice it with the notes spread out in a variety of ways, giving you an *open* voicing (as in Figs. 93 and 94). Some voicings sound better than others in a given situation; experiment and let your ears be your guide.

FIGURE 94

SECTION TWO

CONSTRUCT A MAJOR SIXTH CHORD

All chord construction is based on the *procedure* we used in Section One for the major seventh chord. The only thing that changes are the specific formulas for the different chord types. A major sixth chord is built with the 1st, 3rd, 5th, and 6th scale steps (remember that the root of the chord is 1). Let's build a D6 (sometimes written as D M6 or Dmaj6) chord: see Fig. 95:

FIGURE 95

DRILL
Build the following chords:

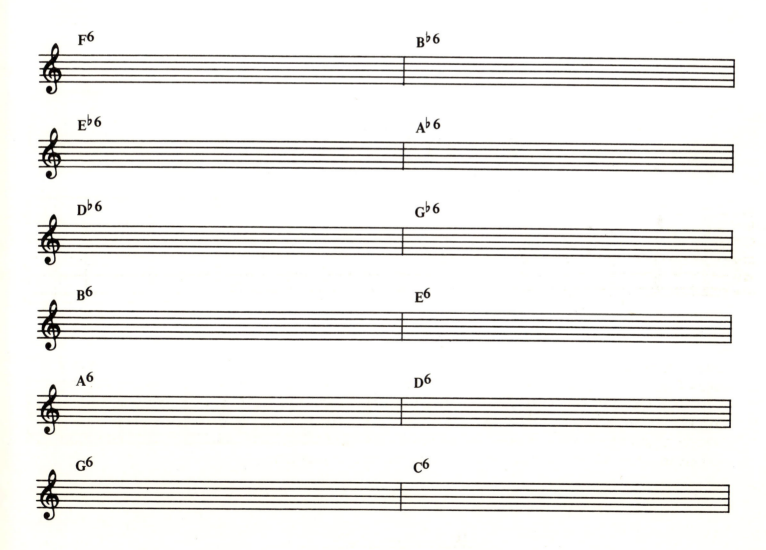

Until now, all the chords we have used in this study have had the roots as their lowest notes (as do most chords you will encounter in your playing career). However, other notes of the chord are sometimes put in the bottom position (or bass). For example, look at Fig. 96 below. The first voicing is the one you learned in Chapter Two, Section Four, with the root of the chord in the bass. The second voicing has the third in the bass (this is called "first inversion"), and the third voicing has the fifth in the bass (called "second inversion"). Play all three voicings. Record them and listen back to them. They all sound basically the same, but the "flavor" changes slightly from one inversion to the next (the terms "flavor" and "color" are used to describe subtle variations in chord sounds).

FIGURE 96

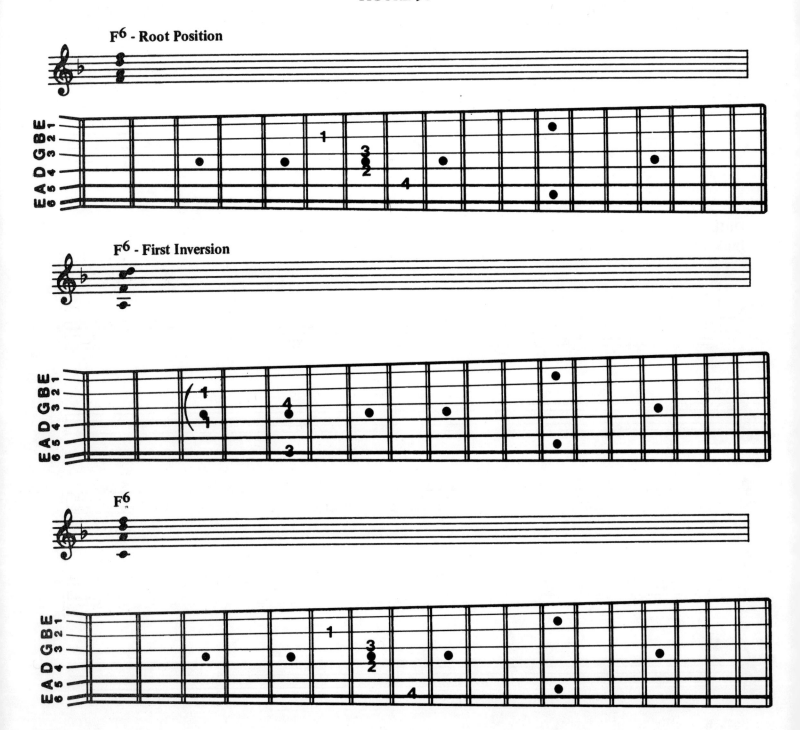

SECTION THREE

CONSTRUCT A MINOR SEVENTH CHORD

As stated in Section Two, all chord construction is based on the principles we encountered in Section One. The only thing that changes from one chord type to the next is what chord steps (such as 1, 3, 5, and 7 for major 7; 1, 3, 5, and 6 for major 6) actually make up the chord.

To build a minor seventh chord, begin as usual: write the scale out with the root (1) of the chord as the tonic (1) of the scale. In Fig. 97 we will build a Gm7 (sometimes written as G—7) chord. As with the major seventh chord, we are going to need the 1st, 3rd, 5th, and 7th steps. However, we must alter two of the notes in order to make this a minor seventh chord: once we know the 1, 3, 5, and 7 (in this case, G, B, D, and F♯), we must lower the third and the seventh by a half step each. Thus the B becomes Bb and F♯ becomes F "natural" or just plain F (♮ is the sign for natural - it temporarily cancels the key signature for that note). Therefore, the notes in a G minor 7 chord are G, Bb, D, and F; and we have our formula for any minor seventh chord: 1, flat 3 (or b3), 5, and flat 7 (b7).

FIGURE 97

DRILL

Build the following minor seventh chords using the above procedure:

(Continued)

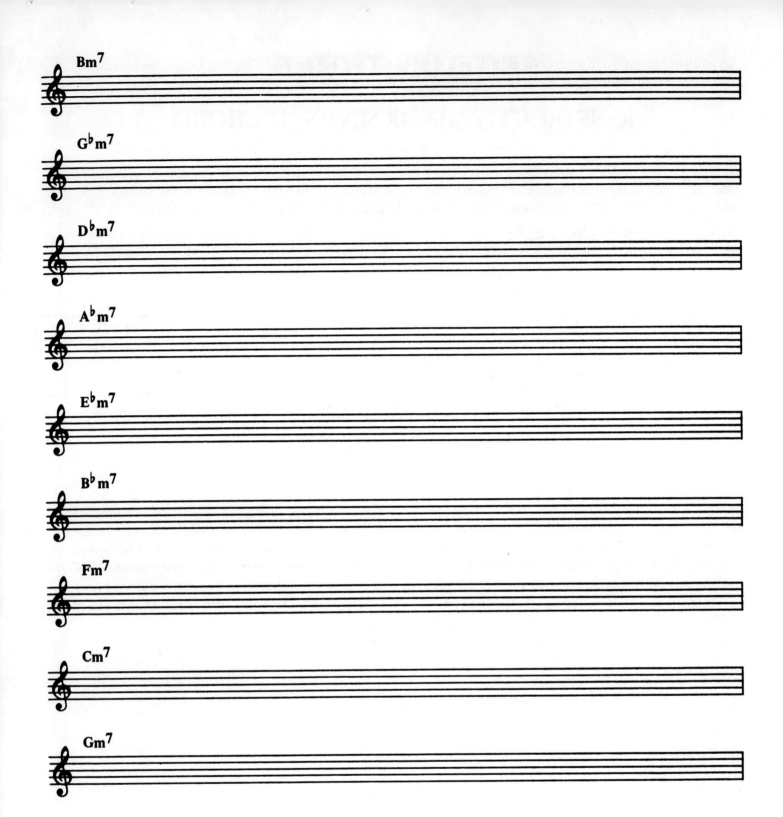

In addition to the minor seventh chords you learned in Chapter One and Chapter Two, here is another standard guitar voicing for a minor seventh chord (Fig. 98 below):

FIGURE 98

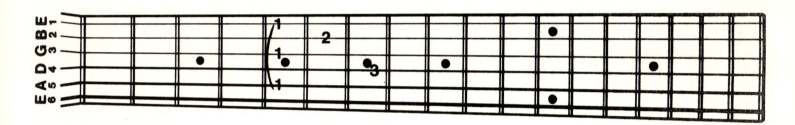

Starting at the root of the chord you have the notes D/1, A/5, C/b7, F/b3, and A/5. Notice that there are two A's in the chord. Does this affect the chord type? The answer is no: any note of a chord may appear more than once in the chord without changing the chord name or function. This is called *doubling* and is used as another device for expanding the sounds available for any chord type. For other examples of doubled chord tones, refer to the chord voicings you learned in Chapter Two, Section Four (root doubled); Chapter Three, Section Four (root and fifth doubled); Chapter Three, Section Five (root doubled); and Chapter Four, Section Five (root and fifth doubled).

SECTION FOUR

CONSTRUCT A DOMINANT SEVENTH CHORD

Using the same procedure for chord construction as in Sections One-Three, you can build a dominant seventh chord. Locate the chordal steps 1, 3, 5, and 7. Now lower the seventh by a half step and you have the formula for a dominant seventh chord: 1, 3, 5, and b7 (see Fig. 99).

FIGURE 99

Build the following chords using the procedure described above:

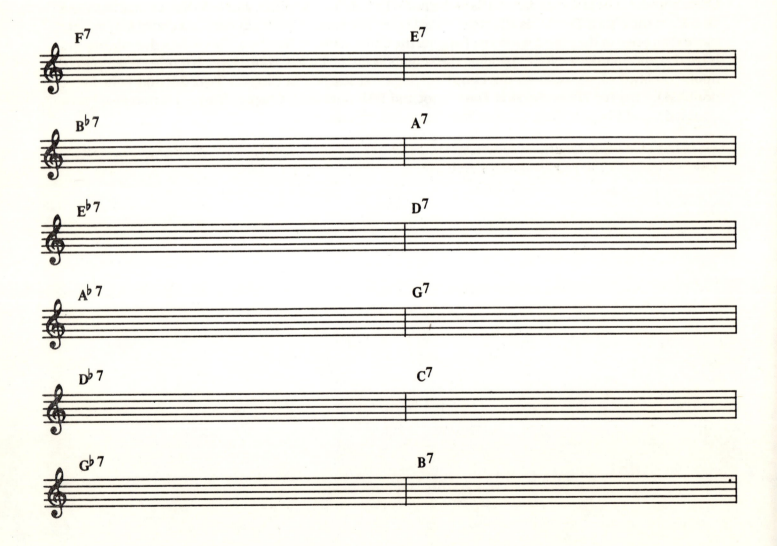

The dominant chords you learned in Chapter One, Section Eight and Chapter Two, Section Five were dominant ninths, not dominant sevenths. Is there some mystical difference between the two chords (for example, G7 and G9)? The answer is no: the G9 is merely a G7 with one note (the ninth, or note A) added. See Fig 100. The addition of the ninth merely changes the color of the chord (for "color" see Section Two of this chapter) without changing the basic chord type or function.

FIGURE 100

The ninth step of the scale has the same name as the second step; it is just an octave higher (if this is unclear, refer to Chapter Six, Section One). In chord symbols, using the name "ninth" instead of "second" tells you that the seventh is *understood* to be included, though it is not specifically stated. Therefore a G9 chord would include the notes G, B, D, *F*, and A (or 1, 3, 5, b7, and 9) while a "G2" chord (less common) would have the notes G, A, B, and D (or 1, 2, 3, and 5: *no* seventh).

DRILL

Go back to the previous drill (building dominant seventh chords). Change all of the chords to dominant ninths by adding the proper note to each one.

CHAPTER ELEVEN-END TEST

Review the instructions for the test at the end of Chapter One. DO NOT GO ON TO THF NEXT CHAPTER until you have completed this test perfectly in the time allotted. Check the overall time limit before you begin, pace yourself accordingly. Review only the information you're not sure of; don't waste time on things you already know

SECTIONS ONE - FOUR
Following the procedures described in this chapter, write the following chords on the staff provided:

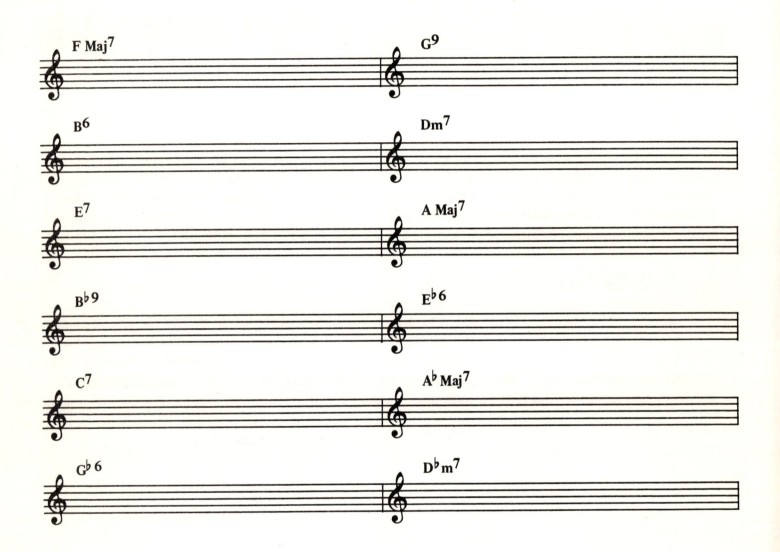

OVERALL TIME LIMIT
30 MINUTES

Chapter Twelve

INSTRUCTION TWELVE:

There is no test at the end of Chapter Twelve; the studies contained in the chapter are a series of tests in themselves and should be treated as such. Remember: speed is *not* of the essence; accuracy is.

Upon mastering the information in this book, you are in a position to undertake any study of music or guitar playing with confidence and a much accelerated learning curve.

SECTION ONE

READING RHYTHMS

In this chapter you will learn the standard notation for rhythms as they appear on the staff. This information combined with the knowledge you already have about finding note names on the staff will allow you to read any piece of music you are likely to encounter.

Look over the information presented with each study below *before* you play it. Make sure you understand completely what you are going to do and what each bit of notation means. Then set the metronome at a slow, steady tempo; one at which you are confident that you can play the study with *total* accuracy. Remember: no mistakes allowed. If you consistently make mistakes at a given tempo, slow down the metronome. Precision is essential in music reading; never go from one study to the next until you have completely mastered the former and can read it with utter confidence.

Studies 1 - 12 are all playable in the scale pattern that you learned in Chapter 8, Section Two.

STUDY #1

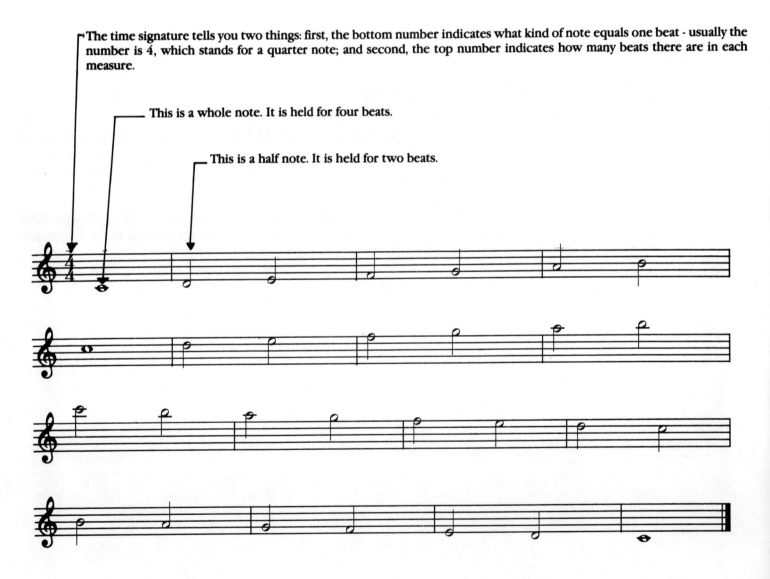

The time signature tells you two things: first, the bottom number indicates what kind of note equals one beat - usually the number is 4, which stands for a quarter note; and second, the top number indicates how many beats there are in each measure.

This is a whole note. It is held for four beats.

This is a half note. It is held for two beats.

STUDY #2

This is a half rest. It shows that there are two beats of silence.

STUDY #3

This is a quarter rest. It shows that there is one beat of silence.

This is a quarter note. It is held for one beat.

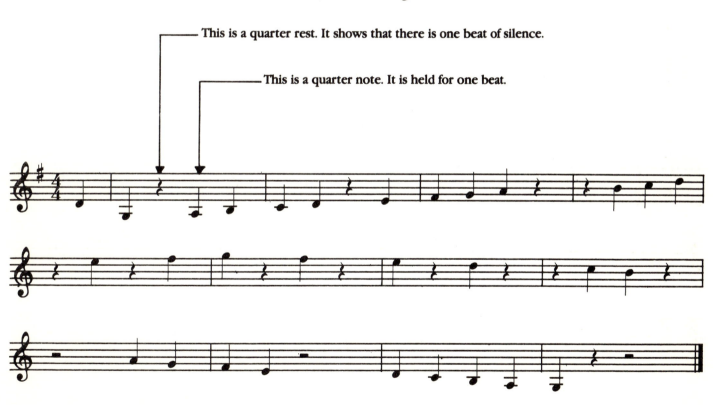

STUDY #4

DOTTED NOTES:
When a dot follows a note, it adds half of the note value to the note.

$$\text{♩} = 2 \text{ beats}$$
$$\text{♩} + \text{♩} = 2 \text{ beats } (\text{♩}) + 1 \text{ beat } (\text{♩})$$
$$\text{♩.} = \text{♩} + \text{♩} = 3 \text{ beats}$$

TIES:
When two notes of the same pitch (i.e. written on the same line or space) are joined with a tie, you attack the first note as usual, but you let the note ring for the combined value of both notes (*do not* pick the second note).

$$\text{♩♩} = 1 \text{ beat } (\text{♩}) + 1 \text{ beat } (\text{♩})$$
$$\text{♩♩} = 2 \text{ beats}$$

STUDY #5

This is an eighth note. It is held for ½ beat; in other words, there are two of them in one beat.

This is an eighth rest. It shows that there is ½ beat of silence.

STUDY #6

STUDY #7

STUDY #8

— This is a sixteenth note. It is held for ¼ beat; in other words, there are four of them in one beat.

— This is a sixteenth rest. It shows that there is ¼ beat of silence.

This is a sixteenth note.

STUDY #9

This is an eighth note triplet. It divides one beat into three equal parts.

STUDY #10

STUDY #11

STUDY #12

Studies 13 - 24 are all playable in the scale pattern that you learned in Chapter 8, Section 6.

STUDY #13

STUDY #14

STUDY #15

STUDY #16

STUDY #17

STUDY #18

STUDY #20

STUDY #19

STUDY #21

STUDY #22

STUDY #23

THE PRAXIS COLLECTION

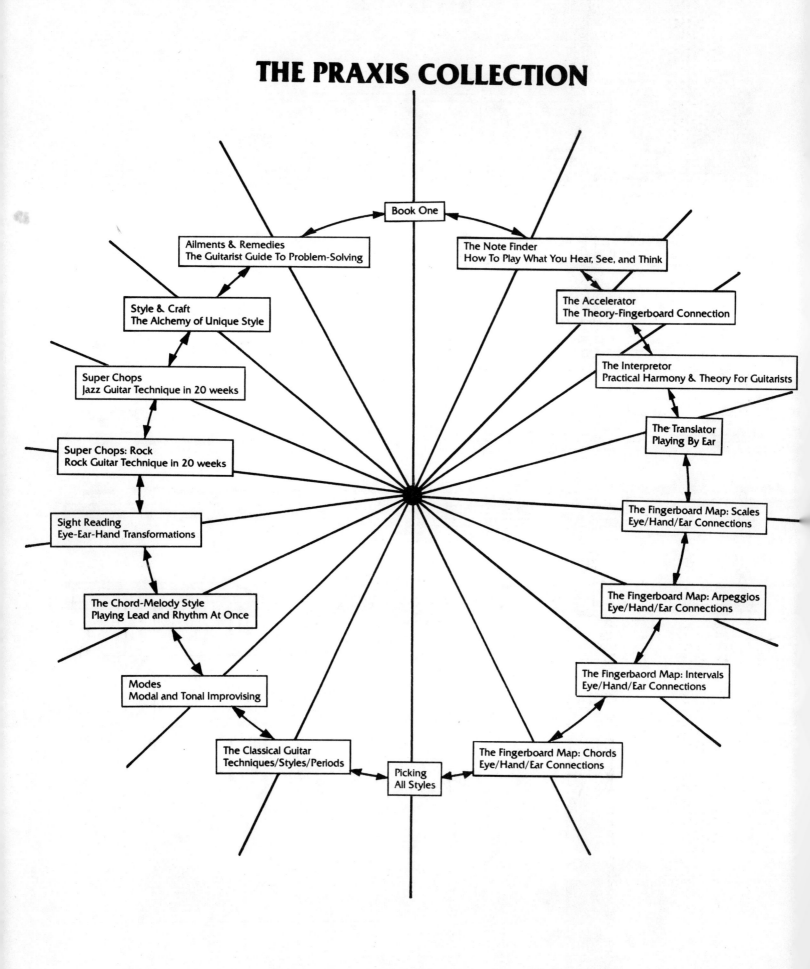

Book One

The Note Finder
How To Play What You Hear, See, and Think

The Accelerator
The Theory-Fingerboard Connection

The Interpretor
Practical Harmony & Theory For Guitarists

The Translator
Playing By Ear

The Fingerboard Map: Scales
Eye/Hand/Ear Connections

The Fingerboard Map: Arpeggios
Eye/Hand/Ear Connections

The Fingerbaord Map: Intervals
Eye/Hand/Ear Connections

The Fingerboard Map: Chords
Eye/Hand/Ear Connections

Picking
All Styles

The Classical Guitar
Techniques/Styles/Periods

Modes
Modal and Tonal Improvising

The Chord-Melody Style
Playing Lead and Rhythm At Once

Sight Reading
Eye-Ear-Hand Transformations

Super Chops: Rock
Rock Guitar Technique in 20 weeks

Super Chops
Jazz Guitar Technique in 20 weeks

Style & Craft
The Alchemy of Unique Style

Ailments & Remedies
The Guitarist Guide To Problem-Solving